FROM SOS TO WOW!

YOUR PERSONAL
COACHING ADVENTURE

MARGARET A. JOHNSON, P.E.

Published by SWOW Publishing
www.ideasandbeyond.com/swow

The following phrases are all trademarked by Margaret A. Johnson:
Heart 'n Smart™
From SOS to WOW!™
Ferris Wheel of Life™
Real Ferris Wheel Deep™
SWOW™

Creatrix™ is a registered trademark of Creatrix, Inc., and Jacqueline Byrd.
Used with permission. www.creatrix.com

Cover design and interior layout:
Anne McLaughlin, Blue Lake Design
www.bluelakedesign.com

Editor:
Stefanie Jacobs, Roo Creative
roocreative@mac.com

ISBN: 978-0-9981295-0-1

First Edition

AS THE SAYINGS GO

I'M SO GRATEFUL

I heard many sayings from my parents and relatives as I grew up, but their relevance didn't really sink in until adulthood. My mom always used to say "ain't my cows, ain't my corn." I'm not sure I understood the depth of it as a child, but now I see the deeper meaning she was conveying with that phrase: that other people's problems do not always need to concern me, or worry me, or in fact they may not be any of my business.

At holidays when presented with dessert options, my Uncle Joe's response was "dessert has no calories" and then he asked for a sample of each instead of limiting himself to only one. To this day, when I am with someone who is debating over having dessert, I share my uncle's phrase and they laugh and usually go ahead and indulge themselves. Now, when presenting others with treats, I tell them they will get ornery and unpleasant to be around if they deprive themselves of life's little pleasures. I like to think that was his point, too.

In our teen years, my siblings and I experienced occasional broken hearts, and Uncle Joe would always try to lift our spirits by saying "men (or women) are like buses, there'll be another one by in ten minutes." He was encouraging us to learn from and laugh about our setbacks, pick ourselves back up and go on. His smart saying can be applied to any difficult time in work or life, reminding us our troubles will pass, we will survive, other opportunities will come our way, and all will be well.

My family's sayings and ways of being became part of me as I grew up. I naturally modified them and adopted them in my own way, and that is also very true with anything I learned from other people — including speakers, teachers, coaches, co-workers, or strangers on an Italian vacation. The list is endless. I see the wisdom of their connection with me as part of my continuous journey in personal growth.

So I would like to take this opportunity to acknowledge many of the influencers in my life whose wisdom touched on the stories I share in this book, and supported me in the journey to create and share *From SOS to WOW!* with you.

I've come across the phrase "burn the boats" in history lessons, online research and most recently in a video clip of Tony Robbins. He was speaking to an audience that included Oprah Winfrey. She loved the anecdote he used to encourage seminar participants to get serious about their goals. It was to burn the boats so

TABLE OF CONTENTS

This book is dedicated to all of those who hesitate and need just a little push (sidekick) to move forward — and to all of those who gave me the little sidekicks I needed throughout my life.

All my love to my family, friends, acquaintances new and old, and those yet to be known!

eHind every super Hero
Here's a super sidekick!

ACKNOWLEDGMENTS

there was no hesitation moving forward, and no possibility of going back to the old ways. In this book, I encourage you to remove the obstacles in your path moving forward and consider how you may be sabotaging your own growth by holding onto the paths that allow you to retreat.

In the realm of professional coach training, mentors, fellow coaches, coaching models — really all things "coachy," I have much to be thankful for. As a professional trainer and speaker, I frequently had individuals and companies ask me to coach them or their employees in a broad range of areas including assertiveness, handling corporate politics and communicating with executives. As a manager, I'd coached my own employees and knew I could help, but wanted to provide coaching in the best possible way, so I set off to obtain my coaching credentials. Countless hours of training, working with higher level mentor coaches, partnering with other coaches, practicing techniques, and applying models have brought me to the place I am today in my coaching journey. But I am certainly not complete. There is so much more to learn and I continue to research, practice, and be mentored. Some of the methods and ideas I've learned from show their influence here, especially in the determination of "where are you now?," "where do you want to go?," and "how will you bridge the gap" along with taking care of yourself so you can be strong throughout your adventure. I like to stay focused on the positives, so the exercise on wants I provide in this book is influenced by the many speakers I've listened to and books I've read that focus on the power of positive thinking, as well as fellow coach Kevin Young who shared an exercise on determining what you don't want, and then pivoting those thoughts to what you do want.

I've participated in training as an employee in corporations, an attendee at public workshops and organizational development meetings, and read many training game books. As a result, I've been exposed to an endless variety of techniques and activities. I have experimented with many of these concepts in my workshops and presentations, much to the delight of my attendees — especially with the change and paper airplane games mentioned in this book.

Early in my married life, a girlfriend invited me to attend a workshop presented by John Gray, Ph.D., the author of *Men Are From Mars, Women Are From Venus*. I enjoyed the material so much that I ended up becoming a facilitator for his workshops — offering couples, dating, and workplace seminars on this communication topic. I am a firm believer in being open to, respecting, and enjoying one another's differences, and I present some gender difference thoughts to reflect on in this book.

When I was working for the electric power company during the late 90s industry deregulation, I had an idea for a class on Risk Taking. Since we were being encouraged to take more risks and innovate, I presented the idea to the Organizational Development director, and was given the opportunity to develop and deliver the class corporate wide. Two of the reference books I used in creating the class materials were *Risk Taking: A Guide for Decision Makers* by Herbert S. Kindler, Ph.D, and *Risk-Taking for Personal Growth: A Step-by-step Workbook* by Joseph Ilardo, Ph.D. I've modified the steps from the former, and described the three categories of personal growth from the latter when writing about risk taking in the book.

There are a plethora of personality and behavioral style tests people can take — including DiSC, Myers-Briggs Type Indicator, Personalysis, Insights Discovery, colors, animals and others — most of which I have completed. The basic premise of personality analyses parameters associated with these tests is referred to in the motivation chapter regarding how different styles are inspired to action.

Dr. Stephen R. Covey, author of *The 7 Habits of Highly Effective People,* encourages us in relationships to seek first to understand and, for productivity excellence, to make planning a focus of our day before jumping into putting out fires. These principles are important reminders for me in my personal and professional life. They keep me out of trouble when I honor them, and get me into trouble when I don't. Enjoy the connection to Covey's work in my book!

When I needed a web site for my business many years ago, I asked friends for recommendations and was introduced to Anne McLaughlin and Blue Lake Design. To my delight, we started with a bartering system — private yoga for web site design — and since then I've grown to be able to pay Anne with real money! We've progressed through web site redesigns and now a book, and I've really enjoyed the journey. After frequent talks with Anne about writing a book someday, and finally deciding which title I wanted to start with, she recommended Stefanie Jacobs to me. Until I hired Stefanie to work as my editor, many of my friends and family wondered if they would live long enough to ever read one of the 50+ books I've talked about writing for so many years. Through patience and rewrites and laughter and tears, and after hours, days, weeks, months and a few years, we are finally here. I am so grateful for their knowledge and expertise and unconditional support, and I look forward to continuing to work with them for many years.

To all my clients — past, present, and future in every one of my many varied work and creative outlets — I learn as much from you as you do from me. Thank you for the opportunity to work and grow with you!

And last but most certainly not least, my family. So many of the experiences I've had, from growing up in a large Catholic family to having my own family and continuing to be outnumbered by men, have provided me with rich and loving life experiences that I am overwhelmingly grateful for. I am sure many of my family members will see themselves and their influence reflected in the stories I've shared within the covers of this book. All my love to all of them — especially my husband, Mike; my sons, Jeff and Michael, and their fiancées Hilary and Chrissy respectively; my mom and dad — watching over me from heaven; and my seven brothers and sisters, Rosemary, Larry, Jerry, Jim, Dan, Berdie, Michael, and their families.

Thank you, friends and readers, too, for all of your positive influences and life lessons, the journeys we have traveled together, and the blessing to be able to influence your lives further by sharing my words here.

— *Margaret (Nutmeg) Johnson*

FROM SOS
TO WOW!™

YOUR PERSONAL COACHING ADVENTURE

SOS is the international signal for extreme distress. Here, it is not that serious, though it may feel serious to some. In this book, it stands for the Same Old Stuff. At one time or another, most people end up stuck doing the Same Old Stuff (SOS) in some aspect of their lives. For example, here we are again …

- ▸ unhappy at work, wondering what else we could be doing.

- ▸ being passed over for a promotion to a coveted position.

- ▸ in a relationship with the same kind of guy or gal we recently separated from.

- ▸ at the gym in January with our stronger, more determined New Year's resolution and jeans that are still a little bit too tight.

- ▶ in a meeting listening to co-workers or your executive team rehash the same old problems with no resolution.

- ▶ watching someone else doing what we have always dreamed about, but not making any progress toward making it happen for ourselves.

The scenarios are endless. Why? We didn't plan to end up here again, right? The truth is, we didn't plan to NOT end up here again.

Whether it is your career, a relationship, personal goals, health and fitness, or your dreams, it's easy to feel trapped in a strange repetitive cycle, running circles with no progress, ending up discouraged when you look at where you are compared to where you thought you would be.

Wouldn't it be better to feel excited and enthusiastic about your situation? That's some of the language typically used to define the word "wow," and once you journey from SOS to WOW, I think you'll experience those emotions. As it applies to this book, I invite you to relate to WOW as being Well On the Way, or as one friend boldly described it to me, "Watch Out World!"

And there's good news. With this book in your hand, you're already on the way. I've written *From SOS to WOW!* to assist you in getting to WOW by providing you with forward moving tips and techniques that you can incorporate into your daily life. With my help, you will learn how to …

▸ get out of the "no progress" repetitive cycle.

▸ achieve your goals instead of wondering how you ended up in the same old place.

▸ make creativity a part of your daily life so that you are able to more effectively solve problems, analyze and take risks, and remove barriers to success.

▸ stay motivated and make real progress toward your dreams and goals.

YOUR PERSONAL JOURNEY FROM SOS TO WOW CAN INCLUDE ANY OR ALL OF THE FOLLOWING STEPS THAT ARE DETAILED IN THIS BOOK:

▸ Seeing where you are stuck and deciding that you don't want to be in that situation any more.

▸ Creating a vision of where you want to be and holding that vision in place.

▸ Determining how you can stay motivated on your path.

▸ Creating Heart 'n Smart™ goals to keep you on track.

▸ Increasing self-awareness and embracing self-care to enable you to get — and stay — on track.

▸ Removing distractions and staying focused on what you need to do to get to where you want to be.

▸ Igniting your creative genius to develop options that help get you where you want to go.

▸ Developing the courage to take the risks/actions you need in order to move to WOW.

▸ Examining your self-talk to keep yourself in a positive frame of mind for success.

WHAT DOES GETTING FROM SOS TO WOW LOOK LIKE?

Every journey is unique, so it's hard to say what yours will look like. What I can say, though, is that with commitment, every vision can become a reality. Here's an example. A young woman was a new manager in a corporation, working for a boss who didn't really know how to build a team; communicate upwards; offer advice on how she could manage her team; or provide any concrete feedback on how she was doing. He always said she was doing "fine" when she asked about her performance. But she wasn't satisfied with her relationship with her manager, her ability to develop the new team, or the overwhelming amount of new information coming at her from all directions. And on top of all that, she was struggling to stay connected with her husband and children because of work commitments. Through her SOS to WOW journey, she was able to solidify a great working relationship with her boss; build a team that could work independently and professionally; feel comfortable in her knowledge of what to do and when to do it; and have a balanced life — with family as a priority.

How did she get there? By working with me through many of the steps detailed in this book:

▸ Clarifying her vision.

▸ Setting specific goals, with the way she wanted to feel being her ultimate motivator.

▸ Increasing her self-awareness and taking better care of herself.

▸ Focusing on one major change at a time.

▸ Busting assumptions that were holding her back.

▸ Brainstorming creative ways to handle situations.

▸ Developing courage and following the steps to more successful risk taking.

▸ Analyzing her self-talk and focusing on making it more positive.

▸ Determining how to stay motivated for the long run.

This book will help you clarify your SOS and WOW situation, and give you the steps and the courage to get where you want to be. In each chapter, you'll find stories, exercises, and tips to facilitate your journey. I've created visual cues throughout the book:

 The stories that look like this are from my personal experiences, and my hope is that they'll help you relate to what I'm saying on your own personal level.

The pages with notebook paper, like this, are your cue to take action. By jumping in to these exercises, you'll start progressing toward your WOW right away.

Approach each of the exercises as a suggestion and feel free to tweak them to fit what works for you. My advice is to try them out — for a day or even a week. You can continue for a longer period if they resonate with you; if not, try out another one.

The reflections and steps to action I've included can be completed through self-study or in partnership with someone you trust, depending how you work best. In many cases, you'll find areas right in the book where you can write down your thoughts and reflections. As you're working through this book, or perhaps when you're done, you may also want to enlist the help of a coach to ensure further success in incorporating changes into your life.

THERE'S MORE THAN ONE WAY TO USE THIS BOOK

Moving from SOS to WOW is a process. Depending on your personality, and maybe even your mood, this book can be approached in several ways.

▶ **Planners** — work through each of the chapters and action steps in the order they are presented for a clearly defined WOW process.

▶ **Spontaneous peeps** — open the book randomly to a page — that will be your chapter and lesson for the moment.

▶ **To-the-point peeps** — review the chapter titles and select the one area you need to work on the most — make that your focus and see your world change for the positive.

▶ **Combination peeps** — pick the chapter topic that fits you best right now and work with it — gradually working through the entire book over the course of time, and checking chapters off as you complete them.

No matter your preferred approach, all readers should begin with the SOS chapter (where are you stuck?), and the WOW chapter (where do you want to be?) since that is the basis for moving forward with success.

Maybe you'll reach your first WOW quickly — with just a challenge or two. Maybe you want to deepen your relationships and all that takes is a focus on being really present with people. Or maybe your journey will involve a longer process and a number of the challenges in this book. Don't worry! Whatever your SOS is, and wherever you want to go, if you take the first step to really focus and incorporate the lessons from this book into your life, I guarantee that you will be Well On the Way to eliminating your SOS. The From SOS to WOW! model on the next few pages provides a visual on how to approach your coaching adventure.

The fact that you are reading this means you are a motivated individual, ready and willing to do what it takes to make the changes you desire. I am blessed and grateful to be accompanying you on your journey to WOW. Let's get started.

FROM SOS TO WOW! MODEL

STEP ONE: READY TO LEAP!

You are reading this book because you are ready. Step one in the From SOS to WOW! model is to determine where you are stuck (SOS) in Chapter 1, where you want to be (WOW) in Chapter 2, recognize your motivation in Chapter 3, and determine your Heart 'n Smart goal in Chapter 4. Then, get ready to jump into action!

FROM SOS TO WOW! MODEL

STEP TWO: THE ADVENTURES!

Focus on your foundation — your way of being — in Chapter 5 before approaching the other topics in full force. Depending on your personality — approach the topics in Chapters 6–10 in order or jump around! Your path to success isn't always a straight line.

FROM SOS TO WOW! MODEL

STEP THREE: WOW!

WOW! You've reached your WOW goals. You're feeling great and ready to celebrate in Chapter 11!

FROM SOS TO WOW! MODEL

STEP FOUR: ONWARD AND UPWARD!

Success breeds success. Move on to your next SOS to WOW adventure in Chapter 12!

SAME OLD STUCK

WHAT IS YOUR SOS?

You know the phenomenon of déjà vu? Where you recognize something in your current experience as having happened before? The words "déjà vu" literally translate from French as "already seen," and when it comes to figuring out what's stopping you from getting where you want to be, that "been there, done that" feeling could be an example of your SOS (Same Old Stuff) behavior.

When my boys were little, they played soccer for many years, delighted to be coached by their dad. At the end of each season there was an all-day barbecue party with field and carnival games for the kids and their families, the highlight of the season for everyone connected to the league.

I remember taking walks around the park on breaks from my volunteer position, to take in all of the excitement and activities. As I looked out over the fields I always felt like I'd been there before: in the same place, with the same people, participating in the same festival, still in my same full time job, year after year.

Each year was different but at the same time, weirdly the same. Maybe a promotion had occurred, but I felt stuck and a bit bored. I knew something was missing in my work but I wasn't sure what I needed or what I could do about it.

I experienced this phenomenon a few more times at the park before I gathered up the courage to make a huge change for the better and started my own consulting business. Those end-of-year soccer events were forever changed for the better.

Where in your life do you keep ending up again and again, wishing it weren't so? While you're thinking about it, I'll tell you about my greatest SOS story. It will help you get to know me a little, and might also serve as an example.

 I am the seventh in a line of eight children. I have five brothers and two sisters, and was raised Roman Catholic, attending Catholic School from first grade through high school.

I can still remember being in religion class in first grade when the teacher was discussing bad behaviors. She asked the class "what happens to us when we are bad?" Oh, I knew the answer to that question and raised my hand frantically, practically jumping out of my seat because I was so sure. The nun called on me and I blurted out "we become the devil." Much to my dismay, I did not get the response I was expecting. I was wrong and it seemed like the whole class was laughing, including the teacher. I was so humiliated. So, what was the "right" answer? Sad. We become sad. I'll tell you what, I was pretty sad after that incident. And quiet. Though that definitely wasn't the only thing to cause me to retreat into my shell as a child, it is the one thing I remember the most vividly. My SOS was being shy and reserved. And it took me practicing a number of self-created techniques over many years to get past it.

I was a good student, but often got marked down for not participating in class. The teachers would always tell my mother: "She is a smart girl. She knows the answers. I just don't understand why she won't recite in class." They didn't know about my pivotal experience in first grade. Still, since getting good marks was important to me, I eventually learned to check my answers over and over and force myself to raise my hand and answer in class. From grade school through college, I had to push myself to participate aloud in class until I had enough points to get my A. But as soon as my grades were secure, I would retreat back behind my books.

I was also afraid to speak in public and would shake at the podium when I had to give reports in school. But again, success was important to me. And so I pushed myself to do it. And the more reports I gave, the easier it eventually became.

Growing up, I always liked boys, but was afraid to talk to them, too. I remember one boy in particular, who I had a huge crush on. I would frequently see him in church (he served as an altar boy), in class, and on the way to and from school. Not wanting to embarrass myself, I decided to make up questions to ask him if he talked to me. That way, when I'd run into him, I wouldn't be tongue-tied. And it worked! I didn't know it then, but the technique of preparing questions in advance is a positive preparation practice that is commonly employed by professionals in any business situation for anything — meetings, interviews, discussions, you name it.

After college, my sisters and I went on a grand vacation tour of several European countries including Ireland. And that is where the magic of the Blarney Stone completed my transformation. We climbed to the top of the tower, and I was held upside down and backwards so that I could kiss the Blarney Stone at Blarney Castle. From that

day on, I was never again at a loss for words. Of course in actuality, the practice of pushing myself beyond my comfort zone for so many years was what got me to my WOW. But it wasn't until I made the commitment to embrace the stone's legendary powers of eloquence that I believed in my own gift of gab. (So don't discount the power of a good luck charm.)

Today, I'm a professional public speaker, and no one believes me when I tell them I used to be painfully shy. But, it is true. So, there you have it. My greatest SOS turned into a WOW (Well On the Way) that gets a lot of HOWs (how did you do it?). It took a long time working through it on my own. But rest assured, not all of your SOS journeys will take that long, especially with the tips and techniques in this book to help you along the way.

So, let's get back to your SOS. You may have several. Which one is at the top of the list for you — the one that causes you the most difficulty and the one you want to conquer first? Think about it. Do you resonate with any of the Same Old Situations here?

▸ Your jeans are just a little bit tight; if only you could lose five more pounds and keep them off!

▸ Your career is at a stalemate and your dreams of climbing the corporate ladder and maybe even running the company one day seem sadly far-fetched.

▸ You dream of doing something big and might even tell people you are going to do it, but never seem to get it done.

▸ You wish you could say no when you say yes, or regret not speaking up.

▸ In meetings at work, you know the ideas being brought up have problems, but you are too afraid to present a view against the majority of the group, so instead you remain silent.

▸ You feel like you're drowning in a sea of clutter and don't know how or where to start to organize and simplify.

▸ The people you work with aren't engaged, and it is affecting morale and productivity.

▸ Your passion is in your business, but the money isn't reflecting all of your hard work.

Is your SOS clear yet? If so, great. If not, or even if you think it is, I invite you to examine the categories of life as an exercise to assist you in narrowing down and clarifying your SOS focus. In the coaching world, the categories are typically represented as a wheel with eight sections, hence the "Wheel of Life." I like to refer to it as the Ferris Wheel of Life.™ You can jump on the Ferris Wheel at any point, work with one of the areas for as long as you want, jump off and get back on to work with a different area of your life. You don't have to work on all of the buckets, just the ones that are important to you. The view is great from any bucket — and it's always changing as you work your way around the Ferris Wheel.

SAMPLE FERRIS WHEEL OF LIFE

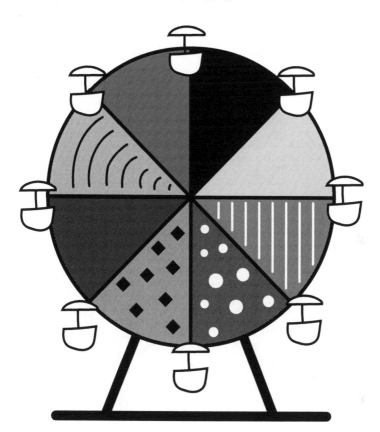

▶ Health/Wellness/Fitness

▷ Romance/Significant Other

◢ Fun/Relaxation/Recreation

◢ Career/Work/Purpose

◢ Money/Finances/Achievement

▶ Family/Friends/Relationships

◁ Environment/Surroundings - Home and Work

◢ Personal Growth/Spiritual Journey/Learning

Create a "Ferris Wheel" for your life. You can use the categories I've listed on the sample Ferris Wheel on the previous page, or adjust them to more accurately fit you. Feel free to add more buckets, or even make a double Ferris Wheel!

▶ _____
▶ _____
▶ _____
▶ _____
▶ _____
▶ _____
▶ _____
▶ _____

For each category on the wheel, consider the view from that bucket and how satisfied you are with that part of your life.

Select the three categories you most want to change in your life, and for each write down

* What isn't right?

* What one thing would make you happier in that area if it were to change?

Is there a common theme to any of these areas? If so, that might be your top SOS. If not, think about the three areas for change you've just identified and choose the one you want to address right now. You can always come back to the others later (and you'll probably find more to add to your "bucket" list over time), but for now, it's important to choose one and focus your energy there.

If you still aren't sure what area of your life to start with, it might be time to go Real Ferris Wheel Deep™ and get more specific with what you really want to change. For example, you might feel like work is the place you would like to start, but you aren't sure exactly what part of work is the issue. By thinking closely about the details, you'll be performing a little root cause analysis — going deep to the root of a problem to solve it. Is there a problem with your relationship with your boss? Are you bored with the actual work? Drilling deeper into what's stopping you with my Real-Ferris-Wheel-Deep methodology will provide you with much needed clarity.

REAL FERRIS WHEEL DEEP
(Career/Work example)

Pick one of the life categories on your Ferris Wheel of Life. Write down all of the specific subjects that fall under that category. There isn't any specific number of subjects required, you can pick as many or as few as you want. Remember, your Real Ferris Wheel Deep bucket will be different from anyone else's because it's specific to you. The Real Ferris Wheel Deep — Career/Work illustration shown on the previous page is an example of delving deeper into the work category of life.

Consider your Real Ferris Wheel Deep SOS and each topic you came up with in that category. For each:

* Why is it important to you?

* What makes you feel like you aren't making progress?

* What barriers prevent you from making progress? What is getting in your way?

* What would you need to do to make progress in this one area?

Does this help you clarify what your real issues are? Now pick one of your answers to serve as your SOS. What if buckets and diagrams aren't your thing? Try selecting a picture in a magazine or a cartoon in a post on Facebook that really resonates with you and visually depicts your SOS. If that works for you, great. Cut out the picture or take a picture of it on your cell phone and keep it in a place where you can refer to it. The point of this exercise is to think about your situation in a way that's meaningful to you, and determine the area in your life you wish to focus on.

Now that you've clarified your SOS, it's time to determine your WOW goal. Once you know both, you will be ready to use the chapters in this book to move onward and upward!

WATCH OUT WORLD!

I'M WELL ON THE WAY

Like the word "wow," being in WOW (Well On the Way) is a wonderful feeling. WOW is the place you really want to be in relation to your selected SOS. As you work to determine your WOW goal, ask yourself this question. If you were "there," no longer stuck in the SOS you identified in the last chapter, and instead Well On the Way (WOW) in that area, what would life look like for you? What makes you want to be there instead of here?

My greatest WOW? Speaking for a living, and loving every minute of it. I am and I do. As I told you in the previous chapter, I shifted from being a shy young girl afraid to speak in public to being a woman Well On my Way. And now it's your turn.

Each journey from SOS to WOW requires a shift. Using some of the examples from the SOS chapter, here's what the shifts might look like:

Your jeans are always just a little bit tight – if only you could lose five pounds and keep them off.

Jeans that look and feel fabulous on you – you only have one size of jeans in the closet.

Shift: Go from being a wisher to being devoted to your health.

Talking about starting your own company and leaving the corporate world.

Soliciting investments in your business, be it on the Shark Tank TV show or in a small business meeting in your home town.

Shift: Go from being a talker/dreamer to getting things done.

Stuck in the same position at work, wanting to get ahead.

SOS

Getting the next deserved promotion to a coveted position.

Shift: Instead of passively doing just what you are expected to do, demonstrating yourself as a strategic thinker who makes suggestions and solves problems both within and outside your organization.

As you think about your SOS, there might be a lot of wishing and hoping and dreaming that things were different around the situation you have. Let's make those wishes, hopes and dreams real.

SEEING IS BELIEVING

For many, visualizing the new you in WOW makes it more tangible and achievable because it helps you see and know where you want to go. Two techniques that I've found work well for this are vision boards and writing.

In many of my presentations and business classes I work with a set of pictures to assist participants in clarifying situations. Picking out pictures that represent the current and desired situations can assist in putting into words the situation a person is experiencing.

To create a vision board, you can use free apps on your phone or computer, pick out pictures from magazines and make a collage, or select a picture off the Internet that really speaks to you on the WOW place you want to be. When selecting pictures, don't pick solely based on images of things you want to have; also focus on the feelings you want to feel when you are at WOW. For example, I have a white convertible on my WOW board. Obviously I don't want to be a white convertible, but I equate driving in that car with freedom, fun, and enjoying the day and the moment, which is the WOW expression I was looking for. I also have a few pictures on my desk. My favorite is a hiker standing a little higher than the viewer, reaching out a hand to pull them up to the next level. I use this as my metaphor for my coaching, speaking and training, since I work with people to raise their performance by lending a hand, and I can imagine the feeling they get when they are able to climb up to the next level.

In addition to using images, you can also write out how things will be for you when you reach your WOW. In the past, I have written out in detail how life would be, how I would feel, and what I would be doing as I reached my next WOW. I find it interesting that many of the things I write out become true as time goes on. In fact, I'd forgotten until recently that when I updated my vision last year, I added that I wanted to be on the cover of Yoga Journal magazine — promoting creativity, risk taking and mindfulness as the path to excellence. When I attended the Yoga Journal Conference this past January in San Francisco, there was a photo booth in the exhibit area where you could get your picture taken and have it put on a mock cover of the Yoga Journal magazine. I jumped in line and soon had some beautiful shots of myself on the pseudo magazine cover. I posted one on Facebook for fun, and to my surprise, everyone believed it was real. But the real shock was when I reviewed my written WOW after returning from the conference and saw the sentence that I had added last year saying I would be on the cover of Yoga Journal! Having a vision can assist you in getting there in many ways, and some may come as a surprise to you.

As you select your pictures or write out your WOW vision, answer the following questions to help you clarify your WOW goal. Make sure the WOW you select reflects the transformation of you out of your SOS situation. :

* If you were no longer stuck in your top SOS and you were instead WOW (Well On the Way) in that same area, what would life look like for you?

* How would you feel differently in WOW than you feel now?

* How would you act differently?

* How would other aspects of your life change positively for you?

* How will you know when you have reached WOW? Is there some measuring stick you can use to assure you are really there?

Using your answers, write down or compile the pictures of your WOW.

Now that you've clarified your SOS and your related WOW, it's time to make your shift. Let's get you into action.

WHEN YOUR "CAN-DO" WON'T

MOTIVATION TO MOVE FROM SOS TO WOW!

So, you are stuck in SOS. Every week, month, or year you find yourself back with the Same Old Stuff in the same old place. What is going to inspire you to finally make some progress toward WOW, and keep the positive momentum going? What will be your motivation?

WHAT IS MOTIVATION?

First, what is motivation? It is the reason behind why we do what we do. I like to test personal motivation in my business classes. When I am setting up the classroom, I tape scratch-off lottery tickets to the bottom of ten chairs. For my introduction to the motivation topic in class, I ask the attendees to please raise their right hand, and most of them always do. I then ask them to please stand up, and most always all of them do. It's amazing how easily people do what's asked (I didn't even say "Simon Says!") and I query them on why they did so. Some reply because I asked them to, and others say because I was polite. There are usually various reasons. I then ask them to stand up and look under their chairs. Participants are usually a little slower to respond, wondering what is up though many follow along enthusiastically.

While they are pondering the request, I add, "would you be more motivated to get up and check under the chairs if I told you there were scratch-off lottery tickets taped to ten of them?" The overwhelming response is "yes!" and before long everyone jumps up and checks chairs for tickets, claiming victory as winners are discovered. In my business classes, I use this example to begin a three-pronged conversation regarding what motivated them; what will motivate them; and whether everyone is motivated. Frequently I hear people say they themselves are motivated but that others, (for example, colleagues and/or family members) are not motivated. I propose we are all motivated. But, we may not be motivated to work on the same desired priorities.

Motivation is individualistic. It varies from person to person. It also depends on the result we are looking for. We may be motivated differently to complete a task at work than we are a task in our home. So, whether it's at home or at work, how do we get to WOW from our SOS? It requires motivating ourselves, and sometimes influencing others. Where can we look for inspiration and motivation? This chapter offers several ways to address this issue.

There is a simple game I use to start many of my business classes to focus a group on the idea of change. The purpose and hope behind any class or training you take is that as a result of the learning, you will make some type of behavioral change for the betterment of you or your organization. This game introduces you to that path of thinking.

To play the game, everyone stands and finds a partner. I then ask them to introduce themselves and respectfully observe each other from head to toe. When they are ready, I direct them to turn their backs to each other so they can't see what the other person is doing, and then change five things about their appearance. They can take things off, put things on, pick things up, put things down, or twist things around. (I let them know that they can only take off so much and still remain professional and I encourage them to *please* remain professional. That always produces a few chuckles as folks struggle to change their appearance.)

People get very creative and a bit crazy in a fun way. I give them a few minutes to complete the task and then ask them to turn back to facing their partners and try to figure out what the other person changed. Once they have figured it out, they sit down.

It is quite hilarious to see the different things my participants have come up with to switch. Not surprisingly, people are nearly always putting items back in their original position as they lower themselves to their chairs, and they continue to readjust once they are seated. Some have completely switched back to normal before they even sit down. It is a rare person who finds the new position for their watch, shirt, or shoes to be comfortable enough to stick with it for the long haul. And that is the point of the game. I reward those who are experimenting with this new way of being and point out their openness and commitment as an example of what to do with all forms of change. We may try out, or even learn something new, but is doesn't take long before we typically choose to switch back to our old comfort zone, if we even attempt the change in the first place. That is why we are all SOS!

How can you prevent that from happening?

First, let's examine why you keep ending up back in the same old place. What barriers are keeping you from moving forward? The answer is as individualized as the person believing and hoping in the WOW dream. Some common barriers include:

- being sidetracked by fear
- a lack of money
- ill health
- too many day-to-day things to keep up with and no time to focus on your goals
- failed past attempts depleting your confidence to try again
- never having the energy to start in the first place

▶ forgetting about the goal entirely as life gets busy

▶ making assumptions about what is (or isn't) possible

▶ no support system or a negative support system

Did I miss any? What are your barriers? Are they assumptions, excuses, or reasons?

Write down three or more things you believe are holding you back. You don't need to spend too much time with them now; we will deal with them later, in Chapter 7. Just have them ready.

Barriers to your success

1

2

3

4

5

WHEN OBSTACLES GET IN THE WAY

There are also obstacles we imagine we will encounter that stop us from taking the first steps. Many years ago, I learned about a game from a Boy Scout story that beautifully illustrates my point.

The scoutmaster had the Boy Scouts set up an obstacle course in a room using the chairs. He had them wind around like a snake with a few scattered in between to block a clear path between them. Once the course was set up, he asked for a volunteer to try to navigate the obstacle course and not walk into any chair while their eyes were closed. Of course, most of the scouts eagerly volunteered for the challenge and the scoutmaster selected one young man to go first. He let the boy study the chair course and then blindfolded him. He spun him around a few times and then pointed him in the direction of the first chair. While he was spinning him, music was playing to drown out any noise the other kids were making. A few boys who were provided insight on the trick of the game were directed to start, and moved the chairs out of the way with the help of the other boys, who soon caught on to the plan.

When the blindfolded boy was instructed to begin, he stood frozen in place. Overwhelmed with all the perceived obstacles in front of him, he was unable to take

the first step. This is indicative of many of the challenges in our lives. Perceived obstacles create a barrier, and fear sets in.

I use this exercise in my business classes to generate discussion around dealing with obstacles and moving forward from there. And that is what this book can do for you: help provide a clear picture of what you are up against, whether real or imagined, and assist you in building the courage to take the challenge and surpass it.

Personally, I love to play golf. The most intimidating part of the game for me is the sand. The more sand traps there are on a hole, the more I think about the sand traps. And the more I think about the sand traps, the greater the chance I will end up in one. On second thought, maybe the most intimidating part of the game for me is the water. The more ditches and lakes and ponds full of water, the more I think about the ditches and lakes and ponds full of water. And the more I think about the ditches and lakes and ponds full of water, the greater the chance I will end up in one. The power of the mind is an incredible thing. So, I focus on the green and the hole, and picture my golf ball dropping into the hole. I am aware of the sand traps and water hazards but I take care to avoid them (as much as I can) and focus on the goal of getting the ball into the hole with the least amount of strokes. I take action — engaging my golf instructor for lessons to learn how to handle the hazards in addition to practice. I know, you're thinking that sounds great in theory, but when I stay focused on my goal instead of my fears; it really does work out for me more often than not. And I know it will for you.

The same is true for any risk we undertake. There will always be hazards and obstacles along the way. Being aware of the hazards means we can take the steps to avoid them or prepare for them as much as possible. Sometimes they will still catch us, especially the ones we didn't even consider, but more often than not we will be successful in spite of the obstacles in front of us.

A project manager I worked with in a class described a plant his company was building in a remote area. In a risk analysis, they had examined all of the possibilities they could possibly imagine could go wrong with the project and created a back-up plan for each possibility. What they hadn't planned for were the cows that happened to get loose from the pasture next to the plant when someone left the gate open. Who could have possibly predicted that one? My client's company was responsible for replacing the lost cattle. But, because they had successfully analyzed possibilities and covered their bases in the planning mode, it was much easier to handle the surprise glitch.

Remember too, that the obstacles that we assume or imagine will pop up on our journey don't always become an issue. So don't get too carried away with planning for them, and don't let the fear of a negative possibility keep you from taking the first step on your journey to WOW.

On the topic of mind power, another common motivation barrier can be the voice in your head. What is it about that inner dialogue that talks you into and out of things? There are conversations that go on in our heads almost all the time, and sometimes the debate is between doing something and not doing it. Maybe you've experienced this internal conflict between the time the alarm goes off and the time you press the snooze button. It is a very short moment but, a lot is said in that span of time. There is a fight going on between the part of you that needs to get up and go off to wherever you need to go to, and the part of you that luxuriates in sleep and wants to enjoy a few more dreams.

 A few years ago, I started training in a form of yoga called Ashtanga (commonly referred to as power yoga). It is a very disciplined yoga practice with a half dozen lengthy series of postures to aspire to. One morning, after staying up late engrossed in a work project, I did not want to get up early to head across town for my yoga practice. Every muscle in my body was tired and sore (and I don't normally get sore), so my body was in some form of shock and denial. I pressed the snooze button. Then I got up and stopped for a short nap on the plush carpeted floor before crawling back in bed after setting the alarm for seven more minutes (as if that was going to help any). My inner fight continued for a half hour. Finally, when the do or die moment arrived — that if I didn't get dressed and jump in the car within the next

three minutes I would surely be too late — some mysterious force took over my body and I was called to action. I did make it to the class on time, I did remember the whole series, I did huff and puff and struggle with the poses and lose a tremendous amount of water through my pores, and I did feel a great sense of accomplishment in knowing that I had made the right decision to go, as hard as it was to convince my tired body to get out of bed.

The next time your mind tells you "I don't want to do whatever it is you are avoiding," take my advice and tell yourself, "Yes. You do." Try it. You will undoubtedly feel better for having accomplished a dreaded task, and who knows, you just might surprise yourself and enjoy what you thought you didn't want to do.

If you need more encouragement to tackle the dreaded tasks, consider the old saying attributed to Mark Twain - "eat a live frog first thing in the morning and nothing worse will happen to you the rest of the day." The frog is essentially your biggest task for the day. If you get that over first, the rest of the day and your tasks will be easier. I keep a toy frog on my desk on top of the most important (and sometimes hardest task) that needs to get done. I tackle that first. It's a great procrastination buster. Consider adopting the frog method.

Speaking of trying, are you trying? Or are you doing? While presenting on creativity to a group of over 200 people at a dinner meeting of quality professionals and project managers, I mentioned a psychological study that found the more creative people *think* they are, the more creative they *actually* are. I then stated we were going to *try* to change their perception of their creative selves and unleash their creative spirit. Then I laughed as I realized my blunder. I explained that instead of using tentative phrases (i.e. "try" and "hope"), they should be confident and say "we will" or "we are going to."

I asked the audience if any of them were ever Boy Scouts and a scattering raised their hands. "Do you remember the Boy Scout motto?" I asked, and a few of those hands dropped. "It starts off with *On my honor I will do my best...* How about Girl Scouts? Any former Girl Scouts in the audience?" Several hands went up. "How does the Girl Scout motto begin?" I queried. "*On my honor I will try...* Boy Scouts will, and Girl Scouts will try," I exclaimed.

This differentiation by sex starts early, but doesn't end there. Through my training and subsequent work with John Gray, author of *Men Are From Mars, Women Are From Venus*, I have become more aware of the tendencies of men versus women in communication. Women tend to make more tentative statements while men make more direct statements, not all, but enough for the data to support the statement. With respect to your SOS to WOW journey (and maybe other areas of your life as well), I believe we all need to "do." So, that evening, I rephrased my statement, saying "tonight we *will* change your perception of your creative self." The group was on board, and we did!

How have tentative statements affected your ability to get things done? Do you follow the stereotypical pattern of your gender with the level of your directness? Is it not an issue for you? How will you use that awareness to move ahead to WOW?

Write your thoughts about being tentative or direct here.

Of course, sometimes trying is just right. When teaching my yoga classes, I always tell my students it is a practice, not a performance. That we are going to try to do the poses and do the best we can, while always backing off if it doesn't feel right. And they *try*. And eventually they *do* the pose. It's a little like the phrase "practice makes perfect." By regularly "trying," you may find that one day you end up actually "doing."

The difference is in the intention of your attempt. Are you trying with the real intention of actually being able to do it someday? If so, great! If not, I trust you will now.

Here's a tip to help move you right now from trying to doing: *decide*. Decide you want to do whatever it is you're working toward, and do more than just try. Commit to it.

Suppose that you want to start your own business, but every day you spend time searching on-line at company websites and career postings like monster.com for a job. You expend precious energy applying for jobs and searching, which is time away from your business dream. If you really want to move ahead with your vision of owning your own business, you have to refocus your energy to stop spending time looking for another job and start spending time on your dream. It's metaphorically referred to as burning your boats.

This metaphor of burning one's boats alludes to certain famous incidents where a commander, having landed in a hostile country, ordered his men to destroy their ships, so that they would have to conquer the country or be killed. No retreating — they were all in.

- ▶ One such incident was in 711 AD, when Muslim forces invaded the Iberian Peninsula. The commander, Tariq ibn Ziyad, ordered his ships to be burned.

- ▶ Another such incident was in 1519 AD, during the Spanish conquest of Mexico. Hernán Cortés, the Spanish commander, scuttled his ships, so that his men would have to conquer or die.

What boats do you need to burn? Are you buying chips and candy, and driving past the gym when you want to lose weight? Do you refrain from asking for the challenging assignment even though you want to get ahead at work? Are you avoiding tough conversations at work or at home when you really want to open communication and improve the relationship?

Make a list of the boats it's time for you to burn.
Beside each, write one concrete step you can
take to really eliminate them and make a commitment to move ahead.

Burn the Boats

* What boats are you holding on to?

* How will you eliminate them and make a commitment to move forward?

* How can you move past the other obstacles
  and make some headway?

THE VALUE OF VALUES

When we are clear on our values, honoring them becomes a motivation. As a coach, it is not uncommon to have clients who are struggling to get all of the things done that they think need to be done. Sometimes people are so exhausted, they can barely get a few hours of sleep a night or have adequate time to spend with friends and family. So what do I suggest? Clarify your values and identify what is important. Doing so provides motivation to take action. Focusing on your values — what is really important to you — may help you find the energy to move forward, and can provide the clarity to eliminate unnecessary tasks.

One corporate executive client I was working with valued:

- ▸ Achievement (many successful customer projects)

- ▸ Safety (for all of the people working for her organization)

- ▸ Communication (open communication between work groups and at home with family)

- ▸ Work/life balance (being successful at work without neglecting family)

- ▸ Collaboration (teams working effectively together)

As she struggled to get all of the things done that needed to be done to start a new division in her company, she was thoroughly exhausted. When she changed her focus to reflect her values, she found the energy to move forward and the clarity to work with her team to delegate as well as eliminate unnecessary tasks. It opened up her schedule for sleep and other important non-work activities. Listening to what was important to her (and why) provided her with the energy to take action and stay focused on where she wanted to take the new organization and her personal life.

Consider what is most important to you. Take some time to think about, and then write down your top five values; the things you hold near-and-dear to your heart. Mine are family, fun, achievement, personal freedom and competition. What might your list include? Family? Tradition? Growth? Courage? Relaxation? Conflict resolution? Excitement? Peace? Spirituality? Friendship? Loyalty? Respectfulness? Tolerance?

As you review your list, consider why each is important enough to be a value for you. How do you feel when you are honoring it? Are you honoring it now, or is it being ignored? What are you doing to contribute to that? What would you have to change to be able to more fully express this value? How does your SOS to WOW journey connect to what is important to you?

Take the time now to complete these questions for each value. I will wait for you.

List your top five values:

1

2

3

4

5

For each value, consider the questions I raised:

* Why is it important enough to be a value for
  you?

* What feeling do you experience when you are
  honoring it?

* Are you honoring it now or is it being ignored?
  What are you doing to contribute to that?

*   What would you have to change to be able to more fully express this value?

*   How does your SOS to WOW journey connect to what is important to you?

Keep in mind as you review your values that just because you are not currently honoring something doesn't mean it isn't important and shouldn't stay on your list. That in itself may be a sign that things need to change. The client mentioned previously is the perfect example of this situation. Focusing on your values can give you the motivation to make the necessary changes to honor them.

In the search for motivation, consider your personality. Each personality type is motivated differently and has different values. Based on psychology, there are four basic behavioral styles that arise, partly from heredity and partly from environmental conditioning. They are typically divided into four personality types, each of which I have listed with its common form of motivation.

PERSONALITY TYPE	MOTIVATION
Driven To Succeed	
Competitive	Competition
Action Oriented	Results
Internal Thinkers	Focus
High-Spirited	
Assertive	Fun
Dramatic	Action Orientation
Spontaneous	Idea Generation
Process-Oriented	
Logical	Process
Rule Followers	Data
Thinkers	Logic
Team-Builder	
Conflict Avoider	Harmony
Easy Going	Empathy
Good Listeners	Consideration

Where do you think you fit on the chart? Do you connect with the motivators listed? There are many tests out there to assess your behavioral style if you don't already know it. Some are available online, while others can be taken from a certified consultant or a credentialed coach. I highly recommend considering your personality and behavior style when selecting a way to get moving toward your WOW.

LOOK BACK TO LOOK FORWARD

History is always a great teacher. We learn from our successes as well as our mistakes. Take a look at the past for ideas to help in the future. At what times have you been successful in making progress on something you've wanted to do? How did you prepare for this in the past? What worked for you? What worked for a while but then failed? What didn't work at all? What was in place that made it work?

Here are some things that have worked for me:

▸ When I said I was going to do something, I did it. Committing verbally to others was a sure fire way for me to get something done.

▸ Taking small steps to success gave me the confidence to take bigger risks. I started writing a blog and the feedback from my writing encouraged me to write books.

▸ Fun is a great motivator. If I could make anything fun, it would make it much easier to get it done.

Consider the tricks and techniques that have been successful for you in the past. How might they help you today? Write down those techniques that worked and those that didn't. What lessons did you learn and what will you move forward with as a success tool?

* Past Successes — techniques that worked to keep you motivated:

* Past Failures — techniques that you've tried but didn't keep you on track for progress for one reason or another:

* Lessons learned — what did you learn from these events? What will you take with you as a successful motivational tool?

ENERGIZE YOURSELF

Attending motivational conferences and/or events can be great a way to get you jump-started. And the good news is there are probably many of them happening in your area all the time. They may include a day-long star studded speaker list with upbeat messages and key points or be a lunch or dinner event with one speaker and a single message. Either way, you're likely to leave the event ready to tackle the world. At least until life happens and you get wrapped back up in your day-to-day "things to do list," awaiting another spark to re-ignite your passion for what you really want to do for yourself and the world. So how do you tap into that energy over and over again and stay on track for your movement from SOS to WOW?

Here is a story, with some tips that work for me, that may help you stay on track and keep that "tackle the world" mentality.

 I feel like I am living the life I want, but even still, it never hurts to do a check-in and receive a little directional boost to continue on your way to WOW. I got Oprah-ed — inspired and motivated by the queen of inspiration! Yes — by the famous talk show host, actor, producer and philanthropist. A few years ago, a friend and I had the opportunity to enjoy a weekend in Houston at the Toyota Center with Oprah Winfrey and her Trailblazers for her "Life You Want" tour.

The Friday evening and all day Saturday event opened with a 90-minute welcome by Oprah, along with her humorous yet moving story and motivational tidbits. As she arose onto the stage during her grand entrance, the LED lights in the neon wristbands each attendee received and wore throughout the event glowed. They started as a beautiful yellow, then turned to an energizing red. Throughout the entire event, our wristbands emitted different colors, depending on the speaker and the topic.

Our Saturday was a mix of speakers including Deepak Chopra leading a meditation exercise, and Elizabeth Gilbert, the author of *Eat Pray Love*, sharing an inspiring story on following your curiosity, which, she advised, can be more inspiring and less frustrating than following your passion. Oprah invited us to work through exercises in our notebooks between speakers, similar to exercises I utilize with my coaching clients. They included creating a vision of the life we want around all of these areas: spirituality, health and fitness, family and friends, home and environment, hobbies, contribution to the world, significant other, career and money.

Of course, Oprah displayed her vision's money section with a billion happy faces emerging from it! (We reflected on this type of visioning in the SOS and WOW chapters at the beginning of the book. If you didn't already go into your particular area of SOS and WOW within it, or don't remember what you came up with, this might be a good time to revisit chapters 1 and 2.)

My girlfriend and I both came away from the weekend feeling energized, motivated and enlightened — ready to tackle the world. On the way home, I asked her what she was going to do with the information. She paused and thought about it, not sure how to proceed with the overwhelming mix of ideas, exercises, and resources to investigate. She decided to commit to working on her wheel of life and vision for her future in each of the areas within it. But, would she be able to maintain the glow without the event to spark her energy every day?

I discovered, while driving home from the weekend, that when it was tapped lightly, my wristband would light up again. To this day, it is sitting on the bar counter separating my living room from my kitchen as a constant reminder of the energy it gives. And, every time I pass that wristband sitting there unlit, opaque and lifeless, I tap it gently on the counter and a beautiful colored glow lights up again for a short time. Some days when I need an extra boost, I wear the band all day. It helps keep me energized and on track to the life I want.

Here are eight smart ideas to help you stay sizzling, not fizzling:

1. **Start right away.** Before you walk away from a training class, inspirational message, event, or chapter in a book, decide on the first step that you will take with the new information you have absorbed. Make a commitment to yourself by telling a friend or writing the commitment into your planner or cell phone calendar. Promise yourself you will do it, and imagine how your life will be if you make this change. Attach some emotion to the action. Connecting a feeling to the new habit will ensure greater success. Don't wait to decide; kickstart your action with this decision.

2. **Create a visual** of how you would like things to be after you incorporate the new information or ideas into your routine. This could be a drawing, a collection of pictures posted on your wall or a poster board, a vision board you create using a computer application, or simply a picture in your mind. Some people find writing out the details to read over and over again more helpful than creating a visual. Make a habit of looking at or thinking about the vision of where you want to be every day.

3. **Make a list.** Make one list of the things you want to happen as a result of the newly acquired event information. Think about the obstacles in your way that prevent you from taking action and create strategies to remove them. Look at the list of what you want to happen every day. Concentrate on moving forward by staying focused on the

positive, and ideas and opportunities will arise to move you along your desired path.

4. **Make a game or a competition for yourself** to incorporate the new ideas into your life or, if this type of activity inspires you to action, compete with a friend.

5. **Keep the training booklet or handout you received** in a convenient place where you will see it every day and be reminded of your new insights. Don't let it get covered up with clutter or placed on a shelf out of sight. The visual reminder will keep you thinking about and processing the new thoughts, just like my Oprah wristband does for me.

6. **Share the information with another person.** Teach and practice with a friend some of the exercises or highlights of what you took away from the event. Repeating what you've learned to another person is one of the best ways to deeply ingrain the information in your mind and ensure you will use it. Create a partnership for WOW by finding someone who wants the same things you do and holding each other accountable.

7. **Schedule time in your weekly calendar** to plan and implement the steps for moving forward. Many people are better able to implement strategies when they make a plan and write it down in advance. Remember the tip on deciding? Scheduling is deciding. Block out the time you need to complete the task on your calendar. That brings you one step closer to it being done.

8. **Hire a coach** to work with you to develop and implement an action plan for your visions and help you to remove obstacles — such as fear, doubt or negative self-talk. I've been nicknamed the "sidekick coach." Even superheroes need support and a metaphorical "little kick in the side" to commit and make the changes that will help them to move forward.

How can you keep things fresh and new and stay on track? What will you do to keep your journey from SOS to WOW new and exciting? I recommend a Joy Journal. In it, keep track of the times you are happy and flowing and really enjoying what you are doing. Make it a point to put more of those activities and moments in your life, knowing the journey to WOW will also make you feel that way. Keep in mind how the activities that bring you joy are connected to the ultimate WOW and use that as motivation to continue.

We've defined where we are and where we want to be and examined our motivation to make the move. Let's take a look at specific steps to get there. The next chapters will assist you in the process of examining the assumptions that keep you stuck (and the ones that keep you from moving beyond the first step), developing creative ideas and ways to bust through roadblocks, gathering the courage and the steps to take the risks required to make progress, and rewiring the mindset that prevents us from seeing what is possible and all of the help that is coming toward us that we just don't see.

IT'S NOT ENOUGH TO BE SMART — YOU'VE GOTTA HAVE HEART!

THE HEART 'N SMART™ GOAL SETTING PROCESS

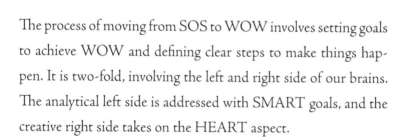

The process of moving from SOS to WOW involves setting goals to achieve WOW and defining clear steps to make things happen. It is two-fold, involving the left and right side of our brains. The analytical left side is addressed with SMART goals, and the creative right side takes on the HEART aspect.

Maybe you have decided on and written out goals before, whether for your professional growth and contribution to your organization's success, or for personal development regarding your health and fitness, passions or dreams. These goals are usually created with a process called SMART, typically utilized in corporate

America, and frequently found in project management. (And since almost everything's a project, the model is universally applicable.) In the SMART process, you clarify what you want and create measurable actions with deadlines.

If you are not already familiar with the acronym SMART, it stands for:

S — Specific Defining a goal clearly so that most anyone can read your description and understand what you are talking about.

M — Measurable The goal is defined in such a way that whether or not you reach it can be determined.

A — Actionable Clearly defining who is responsible for taking action for the goal to be achieved and what needs to be done. (I've also seen **Agreeable** used here, where all parties involved must agree that the goal is a worthwhile place to focus energy. I recommend considering both terms.)

R — Reasonable Ensuring this goal can reasonably be accomplished; in other words, that it is possible. (True, we don't really know until we've tried, but don't let fear get in your way of believing in what can be accomplished in this step. Use creativity to find ways to make the seemingly impossible possible.)

T — Time-framed Having a deadline by which you expect your goal to be reached.

Setting your goals using the SMART process ensures your focus and sets up clear steps to get to the goal. My Heart 'n Smart process is designed to bring you even farther on your path to WOW by addressing not just the specific action steps that must be taken, but also how you want to feel and why. The Heart part helps while you are working toward your goal, and clarifies how you want to feel and be when you achieve that final milestone, which sets up powerful motivators for success.

While working with the Heart part, you will likely discover that your feelings are very deeply connected to the values I mentioned in Chapter 3. Getting in touch with your feelings and writing them out as a desired state of being will provide the Heart piece and give you the motivation to proceed with my Heart 'n Smart process.

 Though I am not in the medical field, medicine and surgery have always fascinated me. A few years ago, I had the opportunity to experience a real "heart felt" situation through a collaboration between heart surgeons and oil and gas engineers, who share their expertise and technology to solve each other's "pump and pipe" problems. I was at a Pumps and Pipes Conference, watching a live feed from an operating room a few buildings away at the Medical Center, and found myself very grateful for the man lying on the table with his chest open. He had volunteered to allow us to view his bypass heart surgery.

The surgeon held the beating heart in his hand and gently turned it on end so that we could see the twisting motion of the left ventricle, like a towel twists when you wring it out. What I remember most are the words of the surgeon as he held the man's heart in his hand: "Isn't it incredible? Isn't it beautiful?" Here was a doctor who has probably seen hundreds, if not thousands of hearts, and still his natural reaction was amazement and appreciation.

I would guess as he set out to become a surgeon, the feeling of what it would be like to do what he wanted was a significant part of his goal process. This man loved his work. And, I want that for you. Whether your work is what you get paid to do 40 (or so) hours/week, or if it's whatever you are doing personally to reach your WOW, I'm here to help you clarify your goals and take the action steps necessary to get there ... by combining the logical SMART process, with the real heartfelt reason you are doing it. Let that feeling of passion be the motivator to keep you making progress on your journey!

Here's another example:

Through the Heart 'n Smart process, one of my clients was able to find time she couldn't, or wouldn't, access before to work with her quilting machines. She had wanted to learn how to use a new piece of equipment for years, and by following her heart, she was finally able to complete a project that had been sitting on the table in her workroom for months. The feeling of joy at finally having the project off the pile, along with having had the opportunity to be creative, really lifted her spirits. To continue to stay inspired, she vowed to focus on the feelings of accomplishment and creativity she had experienced and use her desire to experience those feelings again as motivation to move through other projects. She followed her heart while simultaneously tracking her required action steps with SMART to stay focused on the necessary tasks (in her case, de-cluttering a work space, researching machine training programs, and scheduling time to work) to reach her goals.

Think of a time when you've felt happy, proud or successful. What do you remember about that feeling and how it came about? How did being in that state affect your productivity, enjoyment of your day or your relationships? How much would it mean to you to feel that way again and more often?

Now, let the desire to feel this way again become a very effective tool to keep your goals on track.

FIND YOUR REAL MOTIVATION

Sometimes the feelings you have when you aren't in WOW, but are stuck in SOS, can be motivating in the sense of wanting the WOW feelings and not wanting the SOS feelings. Have you ever considered that frustration can be motivating? If your current situation causes you stress, seeing and believing in the vision of a stress-free life can be inspiring. Maybe it seems like a mind game, but sometimes you have to find a reason that really matters to you in order to turn your goals into reality.

I have been a night owl for as long as I can remember. When I was a little girl I would have sleepovers and we would stay up all night to see the sun rise. In college and beyond, I could easily pull an all-nighter or at least study until the wee hours of the morning to get work done. My energy just flows better in the evening, and I typically get a second wind around 10:30pm.

Recently I spoke about *From SOS to WOW!* at a women's retreat on a Saturday morning. The night before, I had stayed up late making cookies for a friend's birthday and was busy past midnight taking care of other things. I was up early and headed to the retreat with energy and enthusiasm. But in the pictures I was sent of myself that day, I looked tired (even though I didn't feel that way). I don't want to continue to look that way, so I decided to make a commitment of getting to bed earlier with a goal of looking and feeling refreshed all the time. I used the SMART acronym to set my goal, which was easy to apply to getting to bed early.

Specific — Get to bed before midnight every night so that I can get eight hours of sleep in.

Measurable — Look at the clock and see that it's before midnight.

Actionable — Turn off my computer and move to the bed earlier. (And using **Agreeable** — my husband would probably agree that a little more sleep can do wonders for a person's attitude!)

Reasonable — Unless there is a party or special event, going to bed before midnight every night is more than reasonable.

Time-framed — Set a date by which I will consistently be getting to bed before midnight.

So, I set off with my plan, and … it didn't work. I've tried this plan before and it hasn't worked. Why? Because I only focused on the SMART part. So, a few weeks later, I added the Heart part. I attached emotion, desire and heart to my goal plan. I want to feel energized and bubbly and vital and look like I feel that way every day. I have two weddings coming up this next year — both of my sons are getting married — and I want to look and feel especially great for those events (and "happily ever after"). My heart is now attached to my goal. And guess what? Ever since I connected to my heartfelt vision, I've been able to stick to my goals. Heart 'n Smart worked for me. And I firmly believe it will work for you.

Consider your WOW destination.

What is the heartfelt feeling you want? Connect it to your values.

Use the SMART steps to define the specifics:

S —

M —

A —

R —

T —

As you work on the SMART steps to achieve your goal, remember to focus on the heart side — why you want what you want and how it will feel when you get there. Even though they are two distinct approaches, they work together beautifully.

GETTING YOUR MOJO IN FLOW

YOUR WAY OF BEING

Albert Einstein is credited with the saying, "Insanity [is] doing the same thing over and over again and expecting different results." In order to get where you want to get (WOW), you need to change your way of being to get your mojo (your positive true spirit), flowing.

"We've got to get to the water before we leave," my niece's friend pleaded. I was on one of the most beautiful islands I'd ever been to, the Isle of Capri, off the West Coast of Italy in the Tyrrhenian Sea, with my sister-in-law, nieces and their friend. We'd been traveling about the island: walking, taking a bus, and riding a ski lift to see the views, but we hadn't actually touched the water yet. So we made our way down to the tiny cove of rock

and pebble covered beach before jumping on our ferry back to the mainland. My niece's friend slipped off her shoes and started searching on the beach for the perfect smooth rock specimens. Delighting in her finds, she started pitching them back into the water one by one, counting the skips as each one skimmed the water's surface. I tried too, but my stones failed miserably, sinking quickly after a mere half skip or so while she improved on her skip count each time. Satisfied with her last pitch, she watched the small rock sink back into the clear water. Then we grabbed our shoes and headed toward the boat dock for our ride home.

There is something special about standing on the shoreline and skipping stones across the water. The beautiful ripple produced by a perfect skip is mesmerizing to watch, and we all left the beach feeling peaceful, positive and refreshed.

In order to reach WOW, I invite you to make a ripple in the way you do things. Think of the small changes we make in our lives as ripples on the water, awakening possibilities and putting positive things in motion. The changes you make don't have to be huge, but some change in the way you do things must happen for your journey to spark and progress, like the ripple of a skipping stone. Otherwise you will remain in the Same Old Situation. It may be:

▸ Speaking up in meetings at work, where you've previously been silent, for your career advancement.

▸ Going to bed before midnight every night — or at least a little earlier than normal - so you are rested and better able to perform the next day for your overall work or personal performance.

▸ Resisting the temptation to buy your trigger food (i.e. ice cream or cookies) at the grocery store for your health/fitness goal progress.

▸ Taking action instead of talking about what you wish you could or would be doing.

▸ Putting away your cell phone or other distractions and really focusing on what or who is in front of you.

A simple change (though implementing it may not always be simple) will make a world of difference. I have a part time "job" as a fitness instructor, teaching indoor cycle and yoga on a weekly basis. I emphasize this small-change-effect to my cycle class members — "within a minute, a tiny turn of that resistance dial to the right will make a world of difference in the aerobic benefit you will experience as we ride!"

So, where does your change need to occur? In order for you to decide, you need to first connect with yourself and assess how you are operating now. Your habits, presence, energy, and boundaries are good places to explore, and then from there, adjust your way of being.

In Chapter 1 we used the wheel of life categories to assist you in identifying your SOS, and I introduced the concept of my Real-Ferris-Wheel-Deep methodology, using a professional (career/work) example. When I work with clients to determine where they want to begin their coaching, we often start with a visual representation of all of the important areas of their life. Even though clients may come to coaching for work-related issues, their personal and professional lives are intertwined.

To support yourself in moving from SOS to WOW, it is also important to create a strong foundation for your new way of being. Let's examine the different ways of being in your life and break things down for easy analysis and action planning by working through these categories:

1. Caring for Yourself

2. Upping Your Energy

3. Connecting with Other's Energy

4. Staying Positive

5. Being Present

6. Tuning In to Your Intuition

7. Responding vs Reacting

8. Limiting Tolerations

9. Setting Clear Boundaries

10. Practicing Daily Habits

CARING FOR YOURSELF

To build a strong base for your journey from SOS to WOW you must start with you and your well-being. That means examining and supporting yourself, for you are the vehicle for all the change that needs to happen and a distracted, disengaged, dreaming-but-not-doing, or tired, worn out you is not going to get very far. Being aware of how you feel and what is going on around you, and taking care of your needs so that you can be your best, is vital groundwork for the SOS to WOW journey.

I remember being on a spring vacation where the man relaxing on the lounge chair next to me at the pool in the beautiful Mexican town was talking about his company and the work they did. The company sent several hundred employees to this resort for a sales award weekend celebration. An incredible stage was set up on the beach for the evening events and we could hear the music, partying and awards presentation the night before from our cabana nearby.

"Those salespeople that received awards probably log well over 80 hours a week working," he said with pride. He included himself in that prestigious group.

"At what price," I thought to myself, after I inquired about the book he was reading and learned of the separation in his marriage. He had been reading a book about coping with loss, and was taking pride in his work and exhaustion as a badge of honor, but I sensed there was more going on beneath the surface.

We had other conversations when we ran into each other at the beach or the pool, (you tend to see the same people over and over again at an all-inclusive resort), and he openly admitted he wished things had been different, including how much time he had spent working as opposed to on his relationships.

At what price do you run non-stop, all the time unaware and missing out on self-care? Overworking oneself and losing touch with relationships aren't the only ways people push themselves.

 I worked with a personal trainer a while ago — a treat to myself, as I never had one before. I've never been able to do a pull-up and I wanted to kick up my strength a notch and thought a trainer could really help me make it happen. We were working on handstands one day. To practice, you start by placing both hands on the floor with your feet down and your body in an upside down V-shape. The ultimate handstand is a graceful controlled lift to an upside down vertical position, starting with kicking one leg up until the other automatically follows.

My trainer was a very strong guy and he tried to muscle it up on the first one, knocking the wall (fortunately not breaking the mirror) with his feet. We both laughed as he dropped his feet back to the floor. On his second attempt he let it flow and was able to lift up without torturing the wall. It looked, and felt (he said), so much better. It's sometimes astonishing how often and intensely we push ourselves, both physically and mentally. Step back for a moment and reflect on this pushing.

How are you pushing yourself right now?

Is it helping you or wearing on you?

Do you need to find more balance? If so, how could you?

It's true that most people are always taking care of a lot of things and some take pride in their "extremely busy" life. We give, and we run, and we check things off our lists. And then we make more lists before flopping down in exhaustion on the couch or bed at the end of the day.

So, ask yourself, when is the last time you truly took care of you? When is the last time you went out with your friends for some fun and bonding time? When is the last time you took the time for a luxurious bubble bath or a massage to heal those aching muscles? When did you last sit down at a table to enjoy your favorite meal, savoring every bite instead of chowing down while standing over the counter or in front of the television? When have you treated yourself to a glass of champagne or a good scotch, toasting all the goodness in your life with every sip, just because? A walk or run, a new outfit, or a quiet time to read are all treats. The list of ways you could take care of you is endless.

It is important to take care of yourself first so that you have the capacity to take care of the things you need to do and the people in your life. I'll pass on some advice I received once from a coaching instructor. You know the ESC key on your computer keyboard? Think of it as an acronym for Extreme Self Care. Glance every so often at that key, and every time you do, remind yourself to embrace that phrase and consider what you could be doing to really take care of yourself. In fact, I invite you to close this book and do something to take care of yourself right now. Then when you return (and I know you will), make a list of ten additional things you'd like to do to take care of yourself.

Write down ten realistic activities that would provide you with some Extreme Self Care.

1

2

3

4

5

6

7

8

9

10

Now consider, and write down how you will take action on these ideas. Will you make a habit of incorporating a few on a regular basis or pick an item you'll reward yourself with after reaching a particular goal? What will be your strategy for Extreme Self Care? I encourage you to decide and commit to it on paper now. And, remember to refer back to this list when you need some ESC.

Taking time out for you can sometimes be the change in your way of being that needs to happen. Positive changes in our way of being will improve our lives and bring us closer to WOW. Let's continue our exploration of the Way of Being.

UPPING YOUR ENERGY

I teach indoor cycle classes and usually make a new playlist for every class. I select songs that will challenge the group and their heart rate as well as be fun songs to listen to. I always leave that class feeling energized and pleased that I inspired and motivated the group to work hard and enjoy the ride. As crazy as it seems to some people to feel this way about exercise, when my energy is up from class, I feel joyful. Whether that's the word you'd use or not, having positive energy can make a real difference in helping you reach WOW.

Sometimes when I teach yoga, the class comes in all energized and excited with only a few timid first timers. Other times I get a quieter crowd. Either way, I assess the group's energy and frequently, in order to increase their energy level and bring a little joy to their day, my solution is to have them do fun poses like head or handstands. Turning people (and things) upside down is a great way to revitalize attitudes.

For example, one of the preparation forms in the Train-the-Trainer business class I teach is a training requirements questionnaire. It specifies detailed questions that a trainer should ask when developing trainings. But my trainees were frustrated by the lack of information provided by requesters. One attendee suggested giving the form to the requestor to fill out, instead of the trainer doing all the proverbial teeth pulling. Everyone agreed it was a super idea. At the thought of less work and finally finding a way to get the requestor to provide needed information (no complete form = no training), all of the sudden the energy in the room was raised.

Flipping the process doesn't have to just be physical — it can apply to our way of looking at all kinds of things. Changing your perspective changes everything. New insights can up your energy.

Think about your energy and what it needs. What is your typical energy level? What would be a desired way of being for you in connection with energy? Is there anything in your SOS you can turn upside down?

On your SOS to WOW journey, remember to be your own observer and make the energy change to get yourself in the place you want to be. You may find that turning yourself upside down is just the thing to make things right side up!

Another concept to be aware of is your best energy and focus zone. Sometimes people tell us to relax and chill when we are stressed. For some, that's great advice. But it can further stress those types that don't work well in the "chill zone." For some people, a great deal of activity is what de-stresses them, and inaction or relaxation can put more pressure on them. For those people, caring for themselves may have included running, going to a sports bar to watch a football game with team fans or some other higher intensity activity. Others resonate with less activity or a slower pace, and relaxing and chilling is the perfect recipe for de-stress and success for them. Self-care for them might be reading in the hammock. I remember a day when my husband had to accompany me as I ran about town working for a few hours. He said he was exhausted just watching me, yet I was energized by the whole process. Knowing yourself and whether more activity or less is going to be the key for you is a decision only you can make.

So, what about when you aren't stressed but just need a positive boost to your energy? How can you get that? You can get that change from within or by engaging in activities that transition you through to the positive energy you desire.

The singing competition television show *The Voice* does that for me. It is definitely a "feel good" kind of show. It combines tears of joy, excitement, and fun mixed with very talented singers, and watching it makes me happy. When I watch, I forget all my troubles, and find renewed joyful energy that everyone else that I come across after I've watched it tends to notice.

It's true that the feel-good effects of a positive experience might only be temporary, but I believe small adjustments applied consistently will have long-term and wide spread effects. Remember the skipping stone story from the beginning of this chapter and the wave ripples resonating throughout the water. Good begets good. Also, people's energy impacts one another. Energy, whether positive or negative, is contagious. So remaining positive and reflecting positive energy will go a long way in moving you forward on your path to WOW.

Think of a time when you know your energy level isn't as positive as you'd like it to be. Maybe Monday mornings, or when you sit down to pay the bills. Make a mental, or if you prefer, literal reminder to yourself at these times to check your energy and adjust accordingly as a "way of being" modification possibility.

CONNECTING WITH OTHERS' ENERGY

In the same way your energy affects others, others' energy can impact you.

When I go grocery shopping, I always make a point to see if my favorite cashier is on duty, and I get into his line, even if it's longer than some of the others. This checker is the best customer service person I have ever come across in my entire life (wow, that is something to say)! He is cheerful, friendly, easy going, helpful and can calm down the most unpleasant customer with a few words.

I once watched him take care of the customer in front of me as she asked for a bag of ice to be added to her order. The checker walked over to the ice cooler a few yards away, grabbed a bag of ice from the freezer and brought it back to the lady's shopping cart. What service! Even though I have an automatic, working icemaker at home and didn't have any plans that involved filling a cooler with additional ice, I found myself wanting some ice as a result of his happiness to help. When it was my turn, I requested a bag of ice and he purposefully walked over to the cooler and brought me back a bag. I praised his exceptional customer service and told him I had used him as an example in a business presentation I'd given on positivity because this cashier's glass is definitely more than half full.

And I am clearly not the only one who noticed. Though certainly not a reflection of the speed with which he served customers, there was a line forming behind me. I looked back along the faces of the people in line, and they were all smiling — definitely not something you usually see at the store in a long checkout line. The effect a positive attitude can have on others is amazing!

Take a moment to think about the energy around you.

* What words would you use to describe how you feel when the energy you receive from others is up?

* Who are the positive people in your life?

* How can you utilize the energy around you to assist you on your SOW to WOW journey?

STAYING POSITIVE

What is positivity? It is a state of being. It is a way of looking at yourself, your abilities and circumstances and others around you in an uplifting way — noting what is, and accepting it and working with it rather that noting what is not there and complaining about it. Here are two delightful lessons I learned on an Italian vacation that reinforce this positive perspective.

Italian philosophy lesson #1 — My sister-in-law and I were looking for an inexpensive watch battery in Venice. We walked into a Rolex store and knew right away we were in the wrong place. "I think I'm in the wrong place" she said, and I agreed as I followed behind her. Immediately the handsome salesman in a tailored suit with a touch of gray on his temples said "Maybe you are in the wrong place for that (watch battery) but you are in the right place for something else!" We didn't buy a new Rolex watch, but I loved — and still do — his perspective and positive attitude.

Italian philosophy lesson #2 — I was admiring the chandelier hanging above the registration desk in our hotel — it was handmade Italian Murano glass and was truly beautiful — when I noticed a few of the light bulbs were out. So I mentioned it to the hotelier. "Everything is just as it should be" he replied and we laughed. To the Italians, everything is perfect just the way it is because it *is*

the way it is. I love the freedom this thinking brings, and encourage you to embrace it, too.

Too often, we resist rather than embrace. We fight, and complain about and try to fix things instead of accepting them and working with the possibilities.

We all have struggles mixed with good times. Remember: the approach we take makes all the difference. Even when things seem at their worst, there is a positive side. When you look for the good, it's all good.

How do you tend to look at yourself, and others, in everyday situations?

If any of your responses are negative, think about and decide what you will change or do to re-focus with a positive approach.

How will positivity affect your SOS to WOW journey?

Look for the good in your daily life. Keep a record — an energy or joy journal — of when you
are positive and flowing. Take note of what you
were doing when you were feeling up, and what
led up to it. Times when my energy is up and I
am in the flow:

1   Event:
     What led up to it:

2   Event:
     What led up to it:

3   Event:
     What led up to it:

4   Event:
     What led up to it:

5   Event:
     What led up to it:

6   Event:
     What led up to it:

7   Event:

    What led up to it:

8   Event:

    What led up to it:

9   Event:

    What led up to it:

10 Event:

    What led up to it:

As you look at this list, consider how each entry connects to your WOW. I suspect you'll find that they move you closer to your WOW and give you more enthusiasm and motivation to do the things you need to do. How can you keep this momentum going? Look for opportunities to incorporate more of those activities and events into your life, take action to include them, and see how your overall positivity is affected. A more positive outlook will allow you to see more opportunities that will move you on your path to WOW.

BEING PRESENT

There's no time like the present.

So how connected are you to the moment and what is happening around you? Have you ever been driving and all of the sudden you were where you wanted to be, but didn't really remember part of the trip? As if you zoned out or fell into a trance for a few minutes while you were traveling that familiar stretch of the road. Though much of the time it turns out ok, this can be dangerous. We've probably all seen a driver blaze through a red light or stop sign and wondered what they were thinking?

Like distracted driving, I caution you to avoid distracted living. When we don't pay attention, we can go through our day on autopilot, missing out on opportunities around us or barely managing to avoid pitfalls we don't even know we came close to. In doing so, we are not only missing things, but our lack of attention hurts our relationships, productivity, effectiveness, and our ability to get to WOW.

I am a rock n' roll girl from Detroit but I must admit that I have developed a deep affection for country music after living in Texas for more than half my life. One of my latest favorites is a song called "Automatic" by Miranda Lambert. She reminisces about how simple things were before everything became automatic: drying clothes outside on the line, a quarter in a payphone, and recording music from the radio on a tape cassette. It seems people were a little more present in their moments back then, doesn't it?

I was teaching a weight lifting class for another instructor a few weeks ago. As I instructed the class members on each exercise I reminded them to think about what they were doing, how each exercise felt and what muscles were supposed to be engaged. We do things so automatically in class (and all day). When it is time for squats, we pick up the same amount of weight we always do and put it on our bar. When it comes to the bicep curls, we follow along without thinking about the muscles we are working and whether we are swinging our weights or really focusing on the movement. I wanted the group to feel a good soreness in every part of their body the next day because they paid attention to what they were doing, and so I encouraged them to be totally present.

How are you going through your day? Are you on auto-pilot? Or are you really focused and paying attention to enjoy every moment and see opportunity where you might not have before? Turn off the auto-pilot.

It's not just about paying attention when you are engaged in activities, but also paying attention to others and how you are affecting them and they are affecting you. Easier said than done? Yes. So, how can we improve our ability to be more present? One way can be the way we position ourselves.

I find it interesting to observe where people place themselves in a room. When I am teaching yoga, sometimes new people come right up to the front so that they can see and learn the right way to perform the poses. Others, who want to hang back and participate at a different level may set their mat down in the back row or back corner. In those cases, they sometimes get a little surprise when I move to the side or back of the room to lead the class through a few poses and they are suddenly the front row. Making the back row into the front row makes for interesting dynamics.

People often sit in the back at business meetings and group presentations, too. There are a number of reasons people take a back seat at meetings. Some don't want to be called on. Some may not think they have anything to contribute. Others may have work that needs to be done and they don't want to disturb others in the room while they toggle back and forth between listening to the speaker and answering emails on their laptop or their device. But the truth is, by doing something else they aren't totally "there." Try taking a different position in any room you enter and see how it affects your engagement. We are most effective when we are totally present with whomever and whatever we are involved in.

What do you need to do to be more present and effective in your personal and professional life? Think about the things that easily distract you from your focus of being present in the moment. When I am at my computer I sometimes easily switch over to playing a game of solitaire when I am stuck on a work problem to give my brain a break. I've eliminated the game from my icons during my last software update and stay more present without that option available. Working from home, I frequently think about what needs to be done in the house and get up and take care of it. Setting a timer for a specified work period to stay in my seat now keeps me present. What are some of your distractions? How could you eliminate them? Write down a few below and commit to eliminating them, one at a time.

Things I will do to improve my ability to be more present:

TUNING IN TO YOUR INTUITION

Paying attention also puts you in a better position to tune in to your intuition — the things that you know instinctively, or from your feelings. Have you ever had a gut cautionary feeling about certain situations? On the surface everything seems like it is ok but a little voice is telling you something is not quite right and to pay attention. It happens more often than we take notice of. Like the subtle change in your colleague's behavior on a day they are about to turn in their resignation; or a bad vibe from a courtesy van driver in a public parking lot; or a lurking feeling you shouldn't be doing something because the outcome might be disastrous.

It is amazing what we can pick up by observing and being open and receptive to our intuition.

 Once, I was shopping at a department store and as I made my way around the corner of an aisle I noticed the battery display. I had a feeling I should buy a pack of nine volt batteries just in case I needed one for a microphone at the gym. It hadn't happened in years, but I just had a feeling I should grab some that day. Sure enough, the next morning when I went to get the microphone to teach my class, the transmitter was open and the battery slot was empty — no battery! It was a good thing I listened to my gut and picked up those batteries the night before.

I've had feelings about people too. One night on my way home from the gym, I decided to stop at my girlfriend's house and visit. It was not a normal thing to do and I was already tired from a long day but I did. Something told me to turn right toward her house instead of left in the direction of my house. When I rang the doorbell she was so delighted to see me. She had been struggling to help her son with his math homework and needed a break. "Math?" I asked excitedly. Yes, he needed help with math. Math is my favorite school subject and I sat right down and took over the tutoring, much to everyone's delight.

The other day a woman who paid in advance for a cycle class didn't show up to take the class. I wouldn't normally think anything of it, assuming she was tired and overslept or decided not to come. But something told me to check on her. So I sent her an email and found out she had an emergency with her son and that is why she was not in class. She was grateful I wondered about her and I was grateful I'd listened to that inner voice.

But be careful. Sometimes when we are about to embark on an adventure or take a simple step forward, we hesitate and ponder all the options instead. Fear of the unknown can often talk us out of otherwise very positive steps. Still, sometimes there are legitimate reasons to address our hesitations, so it's important to find a balance. Don't ignore your intuition. Couple it with what you know, and do your best to thoroughly and intelligently examine your situation.

When have you ignored your intuition?

If you had paid attention and listened, how might things have turned out differently?

How will you get yourself in the habit of giving your attention to your intuition?

Your gut can also direct you when you're stuck for ideas. Paying attention to it can provide the much-needed guide to your next step. I have a client who is building his business from scratch and is heavily involved in prospecting at this stage. He gets ideas on how to proceed with clients by paying attention to how he feels as he talks with each client and sees how they respond. He uses his intuition as a guide on how to proceed to the next step. Each interaction is unique.

Many years ago I was considering partnering with another training company. I attended one of their sessions as an observer. As the instructor moved in and out of the room between costume changes for a role play I paid careful attention to the audience and my intuition. I picked up on feelings I suspected they had toward the exercise as well as ideas that came to me for changes and improvements. My intuition was key in aiding me in my decision to not work with them moving forward, offering them sound advice on improvements and providing creative ideas for my training techniques moving forward.

* How will intuition enhance your WOW journey?

RESPONDING VS REACTING

Different situations call for different ways of being. Sometimes you need to respond to a situation and for others, it's important to react quickly. What's the difference, and how do you know when to do which?

To me, a reactor is a person who responds quickly and spontaneously, without giving much thought to things. This can be great when there is an emergency. When an accident occurs or something is about to happen, doing what needs to be done immediately to care for or prevent an injury without thinking is appropriate and necessary. I remember responding to a car accident and parking my car on the side of the road and running to help. I placed my hand on the injured knee of the driver to stop the bleeding and a young man who had also stopped immediately ripped off his t-shirt to use as a bandage. We reacted in a positive way.

Sometimes, though, we find ourselves reacting in a negative way. For example when we receive an email at work that upsets us or a driver on the road does something we consider less than intelligent. Emotional situations can evoke emotional responses. Pausing a little longer in situations like those might be more helpful.

Responding involves pausing to assess the situation, and then deciding on the best course of action. It's often based on honoring your values, developing cooperation, and expressing compassion. Being a responder is important when work goals include the best outcome for you, others and the organization. Consider this work example. You are a project manager and one of your team members has delivered key information late and it has affected the deadline. You could start yelling and blaming them for project problems or spend time preparing your thoughts and have a conversation about the issue and how it can be corrected. Responsiveness wins.

In order to maintain peaceful and compassionate relationships at home, responsiveness is important as well. Let's say your kids have the responsibility for certain chores including keeping their rooms tidy. Your son is involved in sports and has little free time after workouts, games, school and school work to do his part at home. You could get upset and threaten to take away sports or other privileges, or work with him to develop a plan where everything is taken care of. The calm responsive "let's work this out" approach is sure to be a winner.

What is your way of being? Are you more of a responder or a reactor? Some personalities seem to naturally pause before they react to things, and others tend to jump right in. Recognizing your tendencies can help you notice when it's time to choose a different style. For example, those spontaneous dramatic personalities may write an email in response to a situation and send it off immediately without rereading it, and then wish they had saved it to ponder over or could retract it. Pausing would have helped them. Conversely, more analytical folks tend to internalize their thought processes and take more time before reacting. Sometimes being a little more spontaneous can help that style.

If pausing is something that would help you, making the adjustment with a technique you can easily incorporate into your life such as counting to ten or breathing deeply, and then analyzing the situation calmly will change your outcomes for the better. The breathing section in the Appendix will help you with this. If a little more spontaneity is in order, consider calling friends up on a whim to go out for a fun activity. Or, the next time you are invited to do something, just say yes without analyzing it. See what happens. It might turn out to be more fun than you expected.

* How has being responsive helped you? What did you learn from those situations that will assist you moving forward?

* How has being reactive helped or hindered you? Reflect on times when it is and is not appropriate to be reactive. How can you improve on your positive reactions?

* How will you be a more effective responder and reactor in the future?

* What will be most beneficial to you as you travel the path from SOS to WOW?

LIMITING TOLERATIONS

Life is hectic, and every one of us puts up with things that annoy or bother us. What kind of things do you tolerate? Here are some issues I've noticed and/or heard others complain about while going through day to day activities:

- negative people

- chronically late car pool mates

- unorganized computer files that lead to wasted time searching for what we need

- so much clutter that boxes or clothes fall on you when you open a cabinet or closet

- things that need to be fixed but remain in their same broken state for days/weeks/month/years

I am similarly amazed at the stories and issues of what frantic or frustrated people write about for help in the well known Dear Abby advice column. Abby frequently responds by saying "it will stop when you stop allowing it." And she is right, it will.

What can you do to stop the things that bother you? Stop putting up with it. Say or do something different to get it to stop. Fix it. Clean it. Do it!

How many things are you currently tolerating in your personal and professional life?

Make a list of them here or in some other type of notebook or computer file that works for you.

Personal life tolerations:

1

2

3

4

5

6

7

8

9

10

Work related tolerations:

1

2

3

4

5

6

7

8

9

10

Take a hard look at these lists and make a plan to start eliminating things. Some can be grouped together and taken care of quickly. Others may take some time.

* What is your elimination plan?

* Where will you start?

* What impact will it have on your SOS to WOW journey to be free of tolerations?

Pay attention to how you feel as you cross tolerations off your list. Do you worry less? Sleep better? Make a note of it. I know when I fix something that I have been tolerating for too long, I feel so much lighter and happier. Start chipping away at your list and see how much better you feel … and how much closer you might be able to move toward WOW.

Tolerations and Boundaries are very closely connected. The first can be a result of not having the second.

SETTING CLEAR BOUNDARIES

When we haven't decided what is ok and not ok with us, and set boundaries for ourselves and others not to cross, we end up tolerating situations that aren't the best. This can make us feel overwhelmed or overworked or just out of sorts and then we lose our mojo. Being clear on our needed boundaries and sticking to them is key to achieving WOW. If we don't, we may end up stuck in our same old stuff with our health, our relationships and our work.

I teach a class for new supervisors and managers and one of the key strategies is to consider how boundaries change as you move up the ladder. Suppose some people were your buddies and now they work for you. Activities you might have participated in with them before or information that you were allowed to share with them has changed. In this scenario, you might want to consider what is ok and what is not ok regarding performance. If an employee is five minutes late, is that ok? What is not acceptable in terms of attendance? What do you do when work quality starts to deteriorate? There are many considerations. It is best to consider how you would handle many of these situations in advance so that you are not caught off guard when they actually do occur. You can't think of everything but you can think about how you would respond in many possible scenarios. It will definitely have a positive impact on your role as a leader.

It is also very helpful to look at boundaries from a personal perspective, considering what is acceptable and not acceptable, and what you will do if someone tries to step over your boundaries. It is much easier to think and plan beforehand than to be faced with the situation and try to decide right then.

As helpful as it is to set and respect boundaries, our boundaries sometimes hold us back from progressing toward our desired goals. Are you keeping yourself from succeeding by forming boundaries or creating obstacles that you think are in your way but when you really come up against them, they melt away or never show up as expected? Or worse, you never discover them because you never took the first step to move toward them out of fear. Maybe you want to write a book but think no one will be interested in it so you put off writing the first pages. Or you dream of owning your own business but never take the time to write a business plan and take the first steps to making your dream come true. Or you hesitate to ask someone out, thinking they wouldn't want to go out with you anyway. Perhaps you imagine that you aren't smart enough or rich enough or fast enough or any number of other fallacies. These assumptions can halt your progress.

Fear often sets up these imaginary obstacles. Our thoughts develop into assumptions and ultimately create our behaviors. Don't let imaginary boundaries and assumptions stifle your creativity and risk taking. I will address those concepts in more depth in Chapters 8 and 9. For now, take some time to consider the boundaries you've set for yourself or the ones you need to set.

Think about what boundaries you have and which ones you need to set up for work and your personal life. List them and then write down some ways you plan to keep them clear.

Boundaries I have:

1

2

3

4

5

Boundaries I need to have:

1

2

3

4

5

Ways I will keep the edges of my boundaries clear:

PRACTICING DAILY HABITS

Habits are regular tendencies or practices — especially ones that are hard to give up. What kinds of habits do you have? Are they healthy or destructive?

I attended a Professional Women's Exchange with the Society of Women Engineers in which an oil and gas industry executive was interviewed on her career and given time to answer questions from the audience. One question posed to her from the audience was, "What were your success habits?" Her top one was not checking emails first thing in the morning. She saw it as a time trap and recommended focusing on other more important things early in the day. This would be an excellent one for all of us to adopt.

What kinds of habits would you like to have? Remember that they don't have to be things you don't like. Habits can be enjoyable activities like engaging in a favorite sport (for me that's golfing).

Here are three healthy habits I believe will support you on your journey from SOS to WOW.

Habit #1: Take Reflection Time

Start every day by taking some time in quiet reflection. Use the time to be creative, relax, or mentally prepare for your day. Before life shifts into high gear, remember that you have the ability to set the tone for the day.

Of course, taking time for reflection can happen any time of the day. This story may help you get there.

 An instructor asked me to teach one of her fitness classes. It was at the same club I was heading to for my yoga class, but there was a 45 minute time gap between the end of her class and the start of mine. No class filled the time slot; there was just an empty room. I agreed to teach for her, and thought I would use the "break" time to catch up on some telephone calls I had been meaning to make.

After the room emptied from the fitness class, I set up my yoga mat and sat down to make my calls. I managed to connect with one person but most of the calls I made ended up with me talking to peoples' voice messages. That was ok. At least they knew I was thinking about them as I left a cheery "hello." I found myself with a half hour before my yoga class started and realized, "wow — here is a full thirty minutes to just enjoy silence and meditate, and I was trying to fill it up with calls and activity."

Not until I took that time did I realize how much I had missed that place where everything stops except the breath. It was a wonderful thirty minutes, and I intend to find more. As each new week or month or year takes

off and so many of us are looking for more, I invite you to look for less. Less stress and tasks to fill your time ... and more awareness and time to enjoy the silence. The places your thoughts will take you and the ideas that never had a chance to grow because of all the activity around them await you!

Find a way to work reflection into your day and enjoy the results. Forming this one habit can really change your life for the better. I've personally noticed the effect in my life. There is less stress when I remember to quietly just observe — to think or not think, and let my mind wander to experience everything that is around me. Use the breathing exercises and techniques detailed in the Appendix to develop your focus skills.

Habit #2: Practice Gratefulness

Forming a regular habit of appreciating what you have is a powerful tool for achieving WOW. Be grateful for those things — no matter how small they are. People who make a habit of expressing gratitude are happier than those who don't, and they are open to receiving more. What does having a gratefulness practice mean? It is being appreciative of and expressing thanks because your situation is the way it is, and it is a positive thing for you. Gratefulness is a way of being that focuses on what is, instead of what is not — like the Italian philosophy lessons I shared earlier. You might be grateful for the farmers who planted and harvested the food you eat, or cared for the chickens that made your omelet possible. You might be thankful you have a job you enjoy when so many others might not like going to work. Whatever yours is, a gratefulness practice involves recognizing what you have and expressing appreciation for it — either silently or to others. Gratefulness practice helps to dissolve feelings of negativity and instead keeps you grounded and open to what else there might be — even to the point you may see your SOS as a WOW from a new perspective!

My gratefulness practice includes making a habit to appreciate the little things in life, like the good cards my husband throws my way in our Cribbage card games, even if I don't win. And the bigger ones, too. I keep a huge quilted heart board from my kids' baby room on the wall of my office and place notes of gratitude on it as often as I feel them. Reviewing the board is one of my weekly habits, giving me a chance to appreciate and embrace all I have, and encouraging me to keep being grateful.

I once heard a presenter suggest using gratefulness to "awaken to your dreams." He recommended thinking about what you are grateful for as you take your first steps in the morning — coming up with one thing for each step you take. See if this technique works to help you incorporate gratefulness into the start of every day.

Be grateful for what you have and you will be blessed with more.

Habit #3: Set Your Intentions

By setting our intention for what we want to accomplish each moment or day, our odds for getting what we want and need rise. Attention, as I discuss in Chapter 6 on Focus, and as Deepak Chopra says, "can be energizing." Intention is clarifying your vision for a desired outcome — and it can be transforming.

I attend a yoga conference in San Francisco every year to renew my spirit and increase my knowledge so that I am able to improve as an instructor. A few years ago I attended a session by my favorite "famous" yoga instructor. She started our workshop seated comfortably on the stage with a beautiful inviting smile on her face. There was a sigh of relief from many of the participants when she said that there would be an hour of lecture, then an hour of yoga. Many of them had already completed several two-hour sessions and possibly a whole day of yoga before that part of the conference and the thought of one more downward facing dog, (a yoga pose in which your hands and feet are on the floor and your hips are lifted so you resemble an upside down V), was daunting. To be able to sit and just listen for an hour to a number of delightful stories was a welcome rest. The instructor shared how "Aim True" had become her mantra. She reminded us of the practice of setting our intention before a yoga class: What were we doing the class for and what

did we want to get out of it? Were we there to relax our bodies? Were we there to heal some injury? Were we there to practice for those who couldn't, or send love and positive energy to those who needed it? In yoga, it is important to set your focus before the class begins so you can direct your energy appropriately...and aim true.

So, too in life, when we set our intention, we are able to get the most out of each moment. If we have a business meeting planned and don't set our intention, how productive are we likely to be? What if we set our intention to really listen and hear what people were saying beneath their words or connect with a person in the meeting that we don't really know? How would that change the outcome?

Set your intention each day and see where it takes you. I guarantee it will create more meaningful experiences for you.

Successful people have successful habits. You've probably heard of Stephen Covey's *The 7 Habits of Highly Successful People*. A number of people have written numerous books on successful habits in many areas — sales, health, executive leadership, and parenting to name a few. Setting up daily, weekly and beyond habits that work specifically for you may be the key to keep you on track to WOW.

It's time to make your own list and come up with a plan for making smart habits part of your reg- imen. Remember there will be ups and downs as you attempt to change your SOS way of being, but small successes will lead to greater victories. How do you think things will change if you make these changes in your habits? Consider that result as you develop and work on your new habits, and see if that future vision will keep you motivated.

* What are your current habits?

* Which ones are serving you that you would like to continue?

* Which ones are not serving you?

* Which ones aren't you doing yet that you would like to add?

* Write out your new list of desired habits.

Daily Desired Habits

1

2

3

4

5

Weekly Desired Habits

1

2

3

4

5

Monthly Desired Habits

1

2

3

4

5

Now that you have a better understanding of all 10 way-of-being categories, what area stands out for you as the place to start? What actions will you take right now to get things on a roll? Do you need to take action in every area of this chapter or just a few? Where will your time be spent the most productively?

If you focus on your way of being and, with your intention clarified, make a change (however small), I promise there will be very positive results for you.

Use the tools and concepts presented in this chapter to give you the courage and direction to make changes in your way of being and ultimately in the positive flow of your mojo. Doing so will be the key to your progress from SOS to WOW. Remember, the journey from SOS to WOW is an ongoing one, and you are instrumental to making it happen.

TAMING THE SQUIRREL

FOCUSING VS. MULTITASKING

Have you ever tried to do two things at once? One night I sat down to watch the Tonight Show, and figured while I was listening to the monologue I would catch up on my Words with Friends games on my phone. What happened? I kept missing the jokes in the monologue as I focused on the games on my phone. And I couldn't come up with any words for the games because I was trying to listen to the monologue. Both activities suffered.

I thought about that the other day when my husband and I took our grand-dog, (our soon-to be daughter-in-law's dachshund) for a walk in the park. We were making our way around the one-mile asphalt track and noticed a runner coming in the opposite direction. He was wearing earbuds and was focused on his phone, with his head down. I kept waiting for him to look up as he approached us, but he didn't. To avoid running into him we would have had to step off into a ditch, which wasn't safe. Instead I ran ahead and waved my hands in front of his face to get his attention. At the last second, he looked up in surprise, and apologized for the near collision. It was definitely an uncomfortable reminder that it's not smart — or safe — to attempt doing two things at the same time!

Having control over your attention is a critical skill. We are seemingly always bombarded with distractions, especially from the digital world. Maybe you believe you are able to successfully multitask and perform several actions effectively at the same time. The truth of the matter is that everyone loses effectiveness, efficiency, and accuracy when they try to do more than one thing at a time.

I believe your full attention is key to making progress in whatever you're trying to accomplish. When you can remove the distractions that take you away from your purpose, you'll stop wasting time switching from one activity to another, and your actions will become much more effective and productive.

Many people never get to WOW because they are constantly putting out fires instead of working on the most important activities to affect real progress. It is true that some of us actually need more stimulation to reach our peak attention/focus zone (e.g., the addition of music in the background), while others work best in a quiet and less stressful environment. But the key is to be mindful of multitasking and use it to raise or lower your energy level when needed, not let it become a distraction from the task at hand.

Single-tasking is focusing on one thing at a time. For example, if you are in a meeting paying attention to the speaker and the questions and responses of those in the room, you are single-tasking. If you are texting or emailing on your cell phone during the meeting, and trying to listen to the speaker or the team as they work through agenda items, you are multitasking. You'll most likely miss out on part of the conversation and/or make mistakes in your texts and emails.

Scientific evidence proves that we can get so efficient at switching tasks that we think we are effective at multi-tasking, but the truth is simple. The brain can only focus on one thing at a time. When multitasking, it tends to go back and forth giving full attention to one situation, then another. And it takes time to refocus on the new task, so efficiency is lost. When we are multitasking, our efficiency and effectiveness are typically reduced by more than 35 percent. The brain needs time to regroup and refocus on the task we are returning to after we are distracted. It can take anywhere from a few seconds up to 15 minutes or more to get back on track. Here's a simple test to prove this to yourself.

Grab a piece of paper, a pen, and a timer. Time yourself as you write down the phrase "I can only focus on one thing at a time" at the top of the piece of paper, put down the pen, flip over the paper, pick up the pen, and write the numbers 1 through 30 in order on the back side. Now time yourself as you alternate writing one letter of the same phrase (I can only focus on one thing at a time) with one number (from 1-30), flipping over the paper between each number and letter you write so that your numbers are all on one side and the phrase is on the other. Remember to put the pen down when you flip over the paper and pick it back up each time you start to write a new letter or number.

How much longer did it take to perform the second task? Most likely at least twice as long, if not much more. That's because your focus was interrupted as you switched back and forth between words, numbers, and sides of the page, and you had to keep refocusing your attention on your task (where you were in the phrase or which number was next). This can be an eye opener as well as a great reminder of how much time is wasted switching from one task to another in your normal workday. If you need more proof of your compromised performance when multitasking, there are a number of exercises to test this in other ways, including short video games and handwritten number and letter exercises. Search for "multitasking versus single-tasking exercises" on the Internet.

So, what can you do to stay focused on and engaged in your task at hand? One method is to make a list of important tasks and block out specific amounts of time to stay on task — not allowing telephone calls, texts, emails, or visitors to disrupt the time block. Taking set breaks after each focused segment to respond to emails or calls and returning to your blocked-out times will make a difference in your overall productivity. For a simple process you can apply to your work or personal activities for better performance, check out www.pomodorotechnique.com. Turning off digital notifications and other interruptions, closing your door, and moving to a quiet, out-of-the way office or area are other simple ways to improve your focus at work.

HOW'S YOUR TO-DO LIST?

Do you have a list of things to do? How long is it, and do you ever really check off everything on it by the end of a day? Maybe it's time to narrow your focus on what you try to accomplish each day by making a big picture list and a daily one. You can also avoid repeatedly moving tasks from one day to the next because you didn't have time to get to it by being more realistic about what you really can accomplish. Another good tip is to schedule some extra time in your day for unavoidable interruptions like phone calls or surprise visits. You might also want to create a back-up plan for yourself, and start on your most important tasks first to prevent unplanned intrusions from becoming a constant excuse. Remember that the ability to effectively multitask is a myth.

Looking for more ways to be more effective? Reflect on what being focused means for you and your work, how you operate now, and what you could change to stay focused and moving in the WOW direction. Commit to it. Right now.

Stephen Covey, author of *The 7 Habits of Highly Effective People*, classifies our activities into four different categories based on varying degrees of urgency and importance. He recommends focusing on the main task of planning: prepare and strategize to keep yourself focused on what really needs to be done, and the rest will fall into place. Spending time in the planning stage sets you up to be more focused and less distracted so that you can really get done what needs to be done! How much time are you spending in the planning zone? Do you need to make a change?

Brendon Burchard, a highly acclaimed author and speaker on motivation and high performance, has a one-page productivity planner that I highly recommend. You can access it on his website, highperformanceacademy.com/vid3top. There is the planner to download and a video to explain the process if you like details. It directs you to pick the three main projects that must be completed in your day and to write out several tasks you need to accomplish to move each of those forward. It also has you clarify whom you are waiting on and who is waiting on you. What calls or meetings need to happen? Working through Burchard's process can really help you hone in on your critical tasks. This is an effective tool for those who are easily distracted by another

SOS — Shiny Object Syndrome (which is when your attention gets pulled away by a "shiny" object or more interesting activity). Of course, it can be a distraction as simple as something in your peripheral vision that takes your attention away from the task at hand. The sweet dachshund I mentioned at the beginning of this chapter exhibits classic Shiny Object Syndrome when she is out in the backyard, running back and forth around the yard chasing a squirrel, a scent — basically anything that moves. It is hilarious to watch, but not so hilarious when we apply it to ourselves, and we are the ones jumping from one activity to another and failing to accomplishing anything at all.

Practicing mindfulness is another great activity that will improve your ability to focus. Here's how to do it:

Start by setting aside some time (it could be 5 minutes, or even 15 minutes) to sit and just be — be alone, be quiet, "be" without having to do anything. Many people find spending time out in nature gives them this opportunity to just be. Try sitting out in your hammock in the back yard or taking a walk in the park. Another coach in my area suggests drawing a dot on the wall and practicing staring at the dot for up to 15 minutes a day to improve focus and concentration. I tried it and lasted only a few minutes the first time. I have some work ahead of me! You can also try yoga breathing exercises to boost your ability to focus. When I first started teaching yoga, I attended trainings and classes everywhere so that I could improve my skills. When I'd go to the classes, I was often stressed trying to get through traffic. But when taking the class, I was able to let go, relax and breathe. As I've become a more experienced yogi, I've learned that the calmness I create in class permeates my being and the more focused I remain, the more the calm feeling stays with me after my yoga session is over. This practice of just being can help you improve your focus and concentration, too. I invite you to review and practice the breathing exercises listed in the Appendix of this book if that is what you are in need of to keep yourself on track to WOW.

Try out several focusing techniques to discover the one that will work best for you. And remember that what *won't* improve your ability to focus and get things done is jumping from one thing to another or paying attention to every alert on your phone or computer. You have to decide to focus and stay focused. Tame your inner squirrel.

Determine your current level of focus. Take some time to think about whether you are able to stay on track on your projects or if you are jumping from one activity to another. To what degree are you accomplishing what you need to do?

How is this current state of being working for you? What needs to change? How would things be if you did make a change? How important is it to you to be in that new state?

How will you make that happen?

Of the tips and techniques mentioned in this chapter, decide which one would be the best for you to start experimenting with and commit to trying that one technique. Make a plan for implementing it into your day and assessing your progress. After a week, reassess your progress and determine if something needs tweaking or if you need to try a new technique altogether.

I do want to add a word of caution regarding focus, and warn against getting too focused on one task without taking time for reflection. It's important to "lift your head up," look around, and stay open for ideas to flow so that you don't stifle your creativity and options. When you are too focused on one thing, it is easy to be oblivious to your surroundings. Participating in a golf tournament not long ago, I did just that.

I was on the tee box celebrating a successful shot I'd made, and my cart buddy was laughing. While I was so focused on making my shot, another golfer's errant ball had landed three feet from me but I was oblivious to the danger of being hit and didn't even hear the other golfer shout the warning, "four!" When I realized the situation, it made me laugh, too.

Balancing focus with awareness applies to personal and professional situations.

I was coaching two executives who wanted to grow their well-established corporate consulting business. One shared his dissatisfaction with a recent airline experience and even detailed the angry letters he had written to the company. I asked if he had considered offering his company's services to the airline instead of just expressing his customer dissatisfaction. He hadn't, but in hindsight, thought that would be a great idea. His focus

on being frustrated with the airline caused him to miss seeing the situation as a potential opportunity for his business.

Sometimes it's hard to remember to look at the big picture. Are you so focused on your current ways of doing or being that you are missing opportunities placed in your lap? Consider intermittent checks from a trusted advisor or coach to help keep you focused yet open to possibilities. Focus on the tasks at hand, but remain open to other ways of accomplishing the tasks.

We will explore how to keep your mind open to possibilities in the next two chapters.

MYTH BUSTERS

BUSTING ASSUMPTIONS, BREAKING BARRIERS

Our ability to move from SOS to WOW most assuredly is stifled by the assumptions we hold regarding our abilities, the behavior of other people, and the options available to us in certain situations.

We all do it. We make assumptions about what we are capable of, what we think people will do or say, and whether or not a new idea, process or approach will work. Assumptions are necessary for progress. Without them we would be stifled indefinitely, waiting to be sure of an outcome. But assumptions can also lead us down the path toward misconception and trouble, with possible damaging results, like inaction or the wrong actions.

As a young engineer, I recall running into my boss' office after hearing an announcement regarding upcoming organizational changes. "Employee Olympics," my former boss exclaimed. That was his nickname for it. "Jumping to conclusions again, are we?" he continued. I laugh when I think about it now. There is a more formal name for this path we follow from initially observing something to selectively collecting data and finally believing what we've assumed to be the truth. It is the Ladder of Inference. I use the Employee Olympics metaphor as a playful way to prevent myself from climbing the assumption ladder.

The ladder process starts with an observation of events. We see or hear something or someone act a certain way. Without really realizing it, we, as the observers, then choose which specific parts of that event we want to focus on. This is referred to as selective reality. Based on this focus, we continue to collect data from our limited viewpoint and make assumptions about what is happening. We collect more data based on this narrow view. We draw conclusions based on that data, and we start to believe the conclusions we have manufactured. In the end we act in a certain way because of what we believe. It is easy to fall into this thinking trap.

Here is how it might happen in real life. A team member from another group is transferred to your group to assist on a project. The team member is quiet in meetings and does not respond to greetings in the hallway. You take that information and selectively look for other instances when the team member is quiet or does not respond to greetings, and discover it happens again. You collect more information when the person exhibits these behaviors, and you start to make assumptions about their knowledge, friendliness and ability to get along with others. You completely ignore the times the person might have been friendly, because that doesn't fit the pattern of the data you first observed and are now focused on collecting. Instead you conclude the team member is not friendly and doesn't know enough about the project to contribute, and you start to treat them as if that were true. You might make the same kind of assumptions about a new neighbor. You have followed the steps on the Ladder of Inference and arrived at a conclusion that you assume is the truth. In fact, the team member could be quiet in meetings and unresponsive in the hallways for any number of reasons that may not match your assumptions at all.

So, how do we remedy this situation? Let's take a closer look at the assumptions we make about ourselves, other people, and situations, and see how we can redirect our thinking.

Have you heard of the bumblebee theory? It is summed up by this quote from Mary Kay Ash: "Aerodynamically, the bumblebee shouldn't be able to fly, but the bumblebee doesn't know that, so it goes on flying anyway."

The bumblebee is a roly-poly creature and from all appearances its wings are too small to allow it to fly. Since no one ever told the bumblebee that it can't, it simply does — in spite of what people might believe. Insect flight aerodynamics are complex and, in spite of having a degree in engineering, I have never attempted the calculations with angles of attack, vortex shedding and other terms that make some heads spin. Scientifically speaking, the bumblebee is perfectly capable of flying. But I prefer to believe the story in quotes. It inspires me (and hopefully you, too) to try things because there's no proof that you can't.

I occasionally share the bumblebee story with my yoga students. I try not to say that "only advanced people can do this pose," or "you are a beginner so don't try this." Instead I tell them to pay attention to their bodies and the messages they are getting. If something doesn't feel right they should back off. They should go slowly into the pose and pay attention to how it feels. I encourage them not to start with the mindset that you can't do something. "Be like the bumblebee," I tell them. "Think 'someday,' not —'no way!'" They stay open to the possibility that they might be able to do many of the poses. And often it turns out to be true. The bumblebee mentality can help you move from SOS to WOW.

What have you been avoiding because you told yourself you couldn't do it before you even tried?

Take a few minutes to think about the assumptions you hold about yourself. (If you are working through this book in order, refer back to the ones you came up with in Chapter 3.)

* Write down what they are here.

* What are some ways these assumptions hold you back and keep you stuck in SOS?

Now let's examine your real capabilities and get you thinking more like the bumblebee. Start by reflecting on your strengths in each of these three areas: your personal strengths, your people connections skills (i.e. relational) and those that you acquired by the experiences you've had (i.e. situational). To assist you, let me share my example.

Margaret's strengths:

Personal assets — I'm trained in analytical skills as an engineer, but am also very creative, so I am able to look at situations with my left and right sides of the brain. I've also found a way to overcome my shyness over the years and am now quite outgoing. These skills contribute to my success as a coach, speaker and trainer.

Relational assets — I'm a professional listener. As a coach, I am trained to listen to not only what you are saying, but what is underneath what you are saying. I pay attention to your body language and the words and phrases you use, and I know how to remove most physical and mental distractions before I coach so I can really pay attention. This helps me in every aspect of my professional work as well as my personal relationships.

Situational assets — I have five brothers, was the only female with a paper route in the area when I was a teen, went to engineering school with mostly men and now have a husband and two sons, so I've been surrounded by men all my life. I believe these experiences have really helped me understand and work with men more effectively than those who might not have had the opportunity to learn the way I did.

Write down some of your strengths in each of these three areas:

* Personal assets — (e.g. confidence, analytical skills, intuition, charm, etc.)

* Relational assets — (e.g. compassion, listening, empathy, tact, patience, etc.)

* Situational assets — (e.g. mistakes that offer learning insights, situations you grew up in, exposure to different languages or cultures, places you've lived in that offered exposure to different opportunities, etc.)

You can take action now, or come back and reflect later on how you will utilize these assets to move yourself from SOS to WOW. The important thing is to acknowledge your strengths, and use them to your advantage.

WHAT ASSUMPTIONS DO YOU MAKE ABOUT OTHER PEOPLE?

I present an activity in my business classes where I instruct participants to raise their hands if the statement I make is true for them. But I tell them to wait to raise their hands until I say it is ok. I query "How many of you like beer?" and quickly remind them "don't raise your hands yet. First look around the room and see if you can pick out the beer drinkers." There are usually a few giggles as people survey the room for people who look like they might like beer. Then I ask the beer drinkers to raise their hands and ask who was right about who they suspected was a beer drinker. Most everyone guesses one or two correctly, but is wrong about most. I continue with more questions for the audience. If there were a horse in the room, who could saddle it up and get on it and actually get the horse to walk or trot? (In Texas we usually have quite a few who are able to do that!) Who is bilingual? Who has a tattoo? My questions go on, and there are always a few surprises. The last question I like to ask is "are you a good dancer?" I ask for a show of hands from the good dancers and ask them to stand. Some do, a few are usually bitten by the shy bug. Then I play a song and ask them to prove it. It always turns out to be glorious fun.

The point of the activity is that people — all of us — make a lot of assumptions about one another and we aren't always correct. But much of the time, we assume we are right, and we act toward that person as if our assumptions are truths. This is the Ladder of Inference coming into play again. I encourage you to recognize the assumptions you are making and test them in some way, just like I did with the dancing exercise.

I stated earlier one of my situational assets is having a good understanding of men. Consider these stories — and the assumptions people often make — about men.

A friend of mine is a wealthy executive. I asked him about his Valentine's Day and he said it was only ok. Apparently he had showered his girlfriend with presents but did not receive anything in return. I commented that just because a person is a millionaire and can buy himself anything that he wants, doesn't mean he doesn't need a little sign of love and affection like a card. "Exactly", he replied.

Men have needs too.

I attended the funeral of a dear work friend who had three children, two sons and a daughter. At the wake, the daughter was surrounded by family and friends. For the most part, the two sons were by themselves, greeting an occasional consoler but mostly talking to each other. One of my friends made an observation that the daughter was receiving a lot of attention but the brothers were off on their own in a corner. Maybe they were more shy than the sister or maybe they needed some attention too. We appreciated our friend for making us aware of this difference, and we each then went individually over to talk to the guys, extending our heartfelt sympathy through words and hugs.

Men have needs too.

In my yoga classes, it seems that the men tend to fall into the strong category and the women fall into the more flexible category. I try not to make assumptions, always encouraging my new students to try each pose and go as far into it as they can. You never know where your strengths are and where you need work in a pose until you try. Sometimes I am working with the men on strength and sometimes I am working with the women on flexibility. I have held up a man's legs so he can enjoy the freedom of a handstand and gently pressed on a woman's lower back to move her deeper into a pose and increase her flexibility.

Men have needs too.

From offending to ignoring, to hurting and much more, think about the trouble that assumption-making can get us into.

How can you stay out of trouble and avoid making assumptions about other people, (including, but not just men)? Keep an open mind. Test out your assumptions. Talk to the person in question, and find out if you are right.

Suppose you need to have a tough conversation with someone, and think they will be difficult. Instead of assuming the worst, look for the best. Start by thinking about that person and finding something about them that you respect. Keep that intention in mind, and believe that they will be open and respectful in the conversation. When you approach interactions in a positive way, you are more likely to have a positive outcome. It is true with conversations, it is true with anything.

STAY OPEN TO THE POSSIBILITIES

Here is a funny story about assumptions and other people and a reminder to stay open to the possibilities.

 I am an avid recycler, to the point that I regularly bring plastic bottles and cans home from events if the venue doesn't have a recycle bin. I keep a large plastic tub in the closet under the stairs just for plastic and had returned home early one evening from running errands. I had my dry cleaning in my right hand, and opened the closet door to lean in and throw my plastic water bottle from my left hand into the bin when the door started closing on me, leaving me in the closet in the dark. I knew my husband was home and assumed he was trying to be funny and trap me in the closet. I started laughing and called out to him. Then I noticed that a strap from one of the newly dry-cleaned tops had wrapped around the door handle, pulling the door closed as I'd leaned toward the recycle bin. I started laughing and came out of the

closet. My husband was across the room, smiling but a bit confused at why I was shutting myself in the closet. When we both realized what had really happened, we had a good laugh about what we'd assumed.

Every event has two sides to it. It's important to remember that our view is not the only possible interpretation, even though, sometimes the stories we imagine are a lot more fun than the reality. Be open to the possibility that your view is not the only view.

Think about these common assumptions about others, and how they might impact you:

At home: You make an assumption about your spouse or roommate and how much he/she will help around the house. If you continue to believe they won't help out, how will that affect the way you respond or react to them? What if you believed the opposite? Would your behavior change?

At work: You make an assumption that your boss would not be open to flextime. You stay miserable with a non-flexible work schedule, missing out on important friend and family activities. What if the opposite were true? How would your behavior change?

Now consider someone or something you believe is keeping you from WOW. Reflect and write down how your assumptions about the person (or people) in that situation might affect your ability to make progress on your SOS to WOW. How can you avoid similar problems in the future?

ARE YOU SMARTER THAN A PIKE FISH?

Situations are another area in which we hold misconceptions about what is possible. Not unlike the bumblebee theory, you might be surprised to learn how many imaginary obstacles you set up for yourself. That process is named the Pike Syndrome and it's based on an experiment involving a Northern Pike that was placed in one half of an aquarium, with minnows swimming freely and visibly in the other half of the tank. The tank was divided by a glass partition, and the pike made numerous unsuccessful attempts to get to the minnows, only succeeding instead in battering its nose against the glass divider. Over time, the pike "learned" that reaching the minnows was impossible. When the glass partition was eventually removed, the pike did not attack the minnows, even though they swam right under its nose!

Don't get caught with Pike Syndrome, which commonly occurs in situations like these:

- ▶ **Ignoring differences in situations** Maybe you have new management at work or other parts of your situation have changed.

- ▶ **Assuming you have complete knowledge about what is going on** Just because you've seen this type of situation before doesn't make it the same.

- ▶ **Holding a rigid view and commitment to the past** Even though the ways of the past have worked for you before, it might be time to try something new.

▸ **Feeling victimized by your environment** Have you convinced yourself that nothing can change because you are restricted by your circumstances (i.e. income, family, economy)?

▸ **Failing to test your perceived constraints** — like the dancing assumption I tested

If you've ever been to an event with pre-set dessert choices, you might be able to relate to this simple example of how (and why) to avoid the Pike Syndrome.

I was seated at the dining table at a business dinner meeting. The table was crowded with plates and silverware, a view obstructing centerpiece, coffee mugs and an assortment of drinking glasses. In front of each place setting was a scrumptious-looking dessert. The desserts alternated with divine chocolate cake at one setting and a traditional cheesecake at the next seat. Unfortunately for the chocolate lover in me, I ended up seated with cheesecake on my plate and sat there eyeing the chocolate cake my tablemate was about to devour.

Instead of resigning myself to the cheesecake, I flagged down a waiter and asked if there was a possibility of getting the chocolate cake instead. He disappeared from the dining area and appeared a few short minutes later with chocolate cake in his hand, proudly delivering it straight to my waiting fork. Other ladies at the table and surrounding tables with uneaten cheesecake sitting in front of them carefully watched every move of the waiter as he delivered the slice of chocolate heaven to my table.

"How did you get that?" some inquired.

"I just asked the waiter," I replied, and told them they could too. You can usually get whatever you want in a hotel. Soon, most of the women around me — and several men too — were eating chocolate cake with devilish grins on their faces. It never hurts to ask.

How many times have you missed out on something because you told yourself that you don't have enough "fill-in-the-blank" to get it done? It's time to get past the many obstacles you believe are in your way.

Write down the obstacles that you think are in your way of getting to WOW, and determine if they are real or imaginary. You may realize the obstacles are only in your head.

1. What are some examples of the Pike Syndrome connected to your WOW journey, either at home or work?

2. How can you help yourself break out of these mental traps?

3. What kinds of behaviors would you like to start or stop doing that would further you on your journey?

4. What are some of your perceived constraints that operate in your workplace or at home?

5. How can you learn to more realistically assess the nature of your constraints and take the steps you need to take?

List the skills and behaviors you believe would be useful to develop as either preventatives or anti-dotes to the Pike Syndrome in your SOS to WOW situation.

What else can you do? Take a hard look at your beliefs and how they affect your actions. Resolve to be open to other interpretations and possibilities. Test your assumptions. For example, do you believe that your hands are tied regarding your work budget, how long something will take, people's openness to change or other options being available to you for your particular situation? What if those beliefs weren't true? How would your actions change? Ask questions and clarify what you believe before you start acting on false conclusions. Practice self-awareness so that you notice when you are starting to climb the rungs on the Ladder of Inference. It will save you a lot of agony and backpedaling, and you will see possibilities for your progress where barriers stood before.

Lately, many of my clients are dealing with the downturn in the oil and gas industry. Some are fresh out of college looking for their first full-time positions and others are dealing with layoffs and the difficult dwindling job market for their skills, while those left behind are disheartened and worried. Small business owners providing services to the energy industry are affected too. Many hold the assumption that until the market picks back up there is no point in trying to find work or make changes, and they are biding their time. One of my small business owner clients was considering postponing promoting his work to the energy industry because of the market, thinking he wouldn't be successful in finding clients. That young entrepreneur changed his mindset after a few coaching sessions with me, deciding that just because there was a downturn didn't mean he should sit back and wait for the upturn. He continued to attend networking events, develop relationships, find some opportunities in energy and explore other markets that he might not have considered before.

SHIFT YOUR THINKING; SHIFT YOUR RESULTS

Here are two examples of myths people commonly tell themselves, and more positive ways to assess the same information, thereby busting the myth.

EXAMPLE #1:

You are a female and want to advance to a leadership position at work.

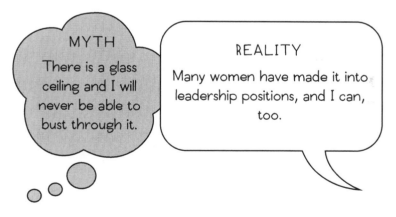

MYTH
There is a glass ceiling and I will never be able to bust through it.

REALITY
Many women have made it into leadership positions, and I can, too.

MYTH

I don't have the skills of a leader.

REALITY

I probably already have many of the skills required to be a leader, and have many opportunities to learn the ones I need to perfect as well as a great support system of people from whom to ask advice.

MYTH

I won't have any support from other women.

REALITY

There are a lot of women's groups I can join for support, and I know or can find women in my company and other companies with whom to connect.

MYTH

I won't have time for my family or fun.

REALITY

I can set boundaries around my work hours and travel commitments, and enjoy my family too.

EXAMPLE #2:

You want to lose 30 pounds in six months and get into the habit of exercising daily and eating the recommended daily allowance of fruits and vegetables in place of processed food.

MYTH

I don't have time for exercise.

REALITY

Exercise doesn't have to take very long. It can be as simple as taking the stairs or parking my car away from the store entrance to get a few extra steps in.

MYTH

Exercise isn't fun.

REALITY

There are thousands of ways to exercise (i.e. swimming, walking, hula hooping, alternative gyms like Cross Fit, canoeing, skiing and other sports) and I can find some that I will enjoy.

MYTH

Vegetables don't taste very good.

REALITY

Vegetables can be cooked many different ways to enhance the flavor; surely I can find some I enjoy.

MYTH

I'll never be able to keep eating healthy after I reach my weight loss goal.

REALITY

Setting up habits to keep myself on track and engaging the assistance of a friend, coach or group support system will assure I stay on track.

What do you tell yourself about why you aren't
in WOW? Consider your specific SOS to WOW
situation. Use my previous examples for direction
and insight.

1

2

3

4

5

How many of those things are really true? What
makes you think they are true? What actions are
you taking or not taking because you think they
are true?

What if the exact opposite were true? How would that change the way you act? Write the opposite of each previous statement and think about how you can act differently.

1

2

3

4

5

Pay attention to the stories you tell yourself — about yourself, other people and situations. Develop the habit of asking yourself these questions regarding your beliefs:

- ▸ What are the stories I tell myself?

- ▸ Are they true?

- ▸ How will I commit to finding out?

- ▸ What if they weren't true? How would I act differently?

- ▸ What will I do differently as a result of this reflection?

- ▸ What will I use as a reminder to pay attention to this? A mantra? An object? Something else?

As you chip away at the beliefs that have held you back from progress, you will find that the outcomes you desire become a reality.

UNLEASHING YOUR CREATIVE GENIUS

PLAYING WITH PATHS TO WOW

As a young girl, I loved math and science, and I still do. I decided in college to follow in my father's footsteps and pursue engineering, encouraged by the market, the plethora of work options, and the pay scale! Looking back at the beginning of my engineering experience, I remember that after four years of working in engineering I transferred to another department and out of my technical group because I didn't feel I had a chance to be creative. At the time, in my mind, the repetitive nature of the calculations I performed and the procedures I had to follow seemed to preclude me from unleashing my creative genius. In reality, engineering is a very creative field, especially when it comes to problem solving. Over the years, I've also found opportunities to unleash my creative side while training people on technical subjects and in my approaches to clients in technical sales.

When people are asked if they are creative, the typical response is underwhelming. "Not really," most reply. How would you respond to the question? Do you believe you are creative? We may not think we are creative because we tend to think of artists or musicians and those in similar professions as being creative, and if we don't fall into that category, we don't have "it."

Many years ago, the owner of a publishing company wanted to improve overall performance and employee innovation, so he hired a consultant to investigate whether his employees were creative. They conducted research and interviewed the employees, and discovered that those who thought they were creative were, and those who thought they weren't creative weren't. It is true. I've experienced the same results myself.

When I give a presentation on creativity, I start by asking for a show of hands in the audience of who thinks they are creative. Not surprisingly, very few hands shoot right up toward the ceiling while several other hands timidly rise up halfway. Most of the class doesn't raise their hand at all. There are various reasons for that; as varied as the people in the room. Some people really don't believe they are creative and others don't want to appear arrogant about their amazing flow of ideas. The truth is that everyone is creative, just in different ways.

Remember, if you think you are creative, you are. If you think you aren't, you aren't.

So why am I making such a big deal about this? Because being creative is important, especially for the SOS to WOW journey. Part of the reason we get stuck in SOS is that we think the ways we have done things, or the options available to us, are limited and there are no new options. In order to move to where we haven't been yet, we must use our creative minds to explore possibilities and come up with (or create) options that we might not have considered before.

Write down 5 ways in which you are creative. Remember, there are countless ways and places to express creativity.

1

2

3

4

5

What prevents you from expressing your creative side? Maybe you don't take the time to let your creativity flow. Or, you used to believe you were creative but don't anymore. How can you get your creativity back? Just start believing. Start believing you are creative and that it is possible to unleash the creative spirit in you. Along with believing, start practicing your creativity.

Here are some simple ways to get started with this. Grab an object in your office or a room at home and sit down with it and a piece of paper and a pen. Write down as many possible uses for that object as you can think of. It can be as simple as a paperclip. Try it now applying the exercise to a pad of Post-It notes. See if you can come up with 25 ways to use the pad of notes. They don't have to be practical. Once you get started, you will find the ideas start to flow. I can think of five right off the bat:

- use several pads like building blocks for children to play with

- post reminder notes around the house for yourself and your kids

- label the dishwasher clean or dirty with a post-it note

- use a small pile of notes for a drink coaster

- use the pads as a game — pile them up into a tower, take turns pulling out one of the post-it pads without toppling the tower (like the game Jenga)

Another creativity exercise you can practice is to look at how you currently do things. Take an activity like planning your day. Come up with three other ways you could approach planning your day. For example, maybe you currently write out all the tasks and prioritize them. What if you split the day into hours and allocated a task for each slot? Or set a timer to see how much you could accomplish before the timer goes off. Or complete the tasks in alphabetical order. Your creative ideas don't have to be the most efficient solutions. The idea is to get yourself thinking differently. And you never know, one of those creative ideas might end up being more efficient after all. Try this exercise with a few things at work and a few things at home. See how creative you can get with alternative ways of operating.

 When my eldest son was in engineering school he enrolled in a required design class. Their weekly challenge was to come up with a new product, investigate it to make sure it didn't already exist, and draft a design to present in class. To assist him in his creative thought process we used to talk about problems and brainstorm solutions. One product we came up with was the "Sun Catcher" — a device for your pool float that would move you back into the shade or the sun while you relaxed and floated around in the pool depending on your preference.

I was reminded of the beauty of this weekly challenge recently when I was walking his and his fiancée's

dachshunds — a four-year-old and a four-month-old puppy — in the park. The puppy occasionally had a hard time keeping up with his fast-paced, squirrel-chasing older sister so I would pick him up and carry him for a little while. It gave me an idea for a puppy carrier much like the baby carrier you strap to your chest with shoulder straps. I was delighted with my new product idea and was ready to jump into designing, producing and marketing it when my son told me someone had already created one and was selling them on Amazon. It was a great idea a little too late.

The concept of thinking about daily problems we encounter and how to solve them is another way to unleash the creative genius in you.

Make a list of 5 simple daily activities you'd like to engage in to increase you creative genius. For the next five days, spend 10 minutes each day practicing a different one.

1

2

3

4

5

The more you play with and practice creativity, the deeper your belief that you are creative will become — and as a result, more ideas will start to flow. Telling your brain to explore new ideas will build your creative confidence and move you toward your desired goals. Think about your situation where you might be stuck in SOS without ideas on how to get to WOW. Creative new ideas can help get you there.

Creative ideas come to you all the time.

* Where do you get your best ideas?

* What are you doing at the time(s) they come to you?

To maximize your creativity, take advantage of the situations when ideas are flowing and place yourself in them more often. Many people find that when they are relaxed and performing activities that don't require much brainpower, their creative genius is in full swing. Some experience enlightenment in the shower; others experience creative genius while driving; and still others while listening to their favorite music or running. Remember to write your ideas down as soon as they come to you. If they are not recorded within a short time, usually 20 seconds, they may be lost forever. Develop a system to record your brilliance. (Note: if you are driving when the proverbial light bulb comes on, pull over to the side of the road to record your wisdom—safety first!)

* How do you record your ideas?

* What else will you try as a method to record your ideas?

* How will you start or continue your habit of preserving ideas? To support your success, I've created a section in the Appendix where you can keep your creative ideas in one place.

I highly recommend setting aside purposeful reflection time to allow the space for new perspectives and solutions. Ideas often come to us when we least expect them, but that doesn't mean we can't encourage openness to new possibilities. Experiment with finding places that inspire you; is it in nature, a quiet space like the lake, a local park, a backyard hammock, or a comfortable chair in your house? For me it is simply sitting in the backyard in a lounge chair by the pool listening to the water cascade from the hot tub to the pool or escaping to the beach a short drive down the freeway for a few hours and spending time just watching the waves or walking along the shoreline.

If you don't already have one, consider creating a space in your backyard or in your home where you can spend some quiet reflection time. After we kids were all grown up and out of the house, my parents put my grandparents' wicker furniture from the farm house in the boys' former bedroom upstairs and created a sitting room. I loved to go up there to read or just relax when I was back home visiting. Now that furniture is in my house — some in my office and some upstairs in a bedroom. I find sitting in the rocking chair or on the couch very relaxing and idea-generating.

Pay attention to what centers you, and make time in your schedule to get to those places. Give yourself time to create. Sometimes your mind just needs a break from all the other things going on in there. Give yourself a chance to think casually and calmly about nothing. And then, maybe, nothing will become something.

GIVE YOURSELF PHYSICAL ROOM TO CREATE

Have you ever opened a closet or cabinet to place another item in it, and been knocked on the head by falling umbrellas or dishes? Do you have a file cabinet at work or home that you keep stuffing papers into, or a file on your computer that you regularly move information into without ever taking the time to de-clutter and reorganize? How can you think when stuff is falling down around you? When your office or your home is full of things that you don't really need, it is time for an overhaul.

The simple act of throwing something away can lift your spirits and clear your head for creative ideas to flow. Many people don't ever start on this because it seems like an overwhelming task to de-clutter. They assume it will take hours or days to make an impact and that they don't have the time to do it right now. So they keep waiting for the day when they will have that precious break in their hectic schedule. But it never comes. And the creative ideas stay stuck in their heads along with the clutter in their environment.

The solution? Start small. Starting small — and just starting at all — are the ways to make your overhaul happen. Dump a drawer upside down on the floor or counter, pull all of your clothes off a closet rod, or open up that file cabinet at work (whether it's physical or virtual) and start sifting. Commit to fifteen minutes a day and you'll delight in the difference a little bit at a time can make.

We recently had our whole house painted, including the garage and I was thrilled to be de-cluttering each room as the painter made his way through the house. The most significant area was the garage. Everything had to come out so the floor could be painted, and years of collected tools, gardening and outdoor stuff turned into an empty garage floor. It was the best feeling in the world!

Organizing a personal or work space that you've wanted to take care of is good for your creativity. When you open up space by de-cluttering, it makes space for new ideas to get in.

The power of de-cluttering applies to your schedule and all the things you have on your mind that sometimes keep your head spinning, too. Mental clutter can prevent our creativity from flowing as much, if not more than the physical stuff. So look for ways to organize your thoughts. Are you doing too much and need a break? Do you need to delegate more at home (or work) so that you have more time for the important things?

BEWARE THE IDEA SMASHER

I used to love watching The Tonight Show with Jay Leno and was intrigued by one of the segments he aired about a product-invention company called Quirky.com. If an idea posted on their site gains a certain amount of attention and positive feedback, the Quirky Company produces and markets the product, and the inventor reaps a portion of the profits. They also post ideas that still might need a little work and invite website visitors to offer their insight. I think it's a great way to get an idea to market when you don't have the initial resources or the know-how, and my creative juices started flowing. So I mentioned that I wanted to submit some ideas to Quirky to a guy at the gym I know who always seems to have a solution to problems or a gadget in mind to fix them. He initially burst my bubble of enthusiasm, saying that "ideas are a dime a dozen" but I stood my ground, and after I shared a few successful products ideas from the show, his cynicism tempered.

There will always be cynics and idea- and enthusiasm-smashers (like the "friend" who initially squelched my interest in Quirky. com) who trash our ideas, or shake their heads, or give us less-than-enthusiastic responses when we reveal our latest crazy dream. Don't let them bring you down. Your creative ideas are important, and if you want to pursue a dream, you can't afford to be stopped by nay-sayers. Here are some ways to handle potential critics:

- Don't share your ideas with them; instead find a more supportive audience.

- Share your ideas, but ignore any negative response they might have.

- Ask what they like about your idea, what they might change, or what part of the idea causes them concern, and then politely ask for any suggestions.

I particularly like the last approach. Hearing what others think about your ideas can help you build on and improve your vision. It is also a great reminder to ourselves on how to behave when someone approaches us with an idea. Pause first before reacting to their idea. Think about what parts of the idea you like, what you are concerned about, and what suggestions you have for improving on it. Either way, you or they might end up with a better idea and someone on your side.

MINUTES, NOT HOURS

Maybe you don't have hours of time to set aside looking for creativity. I started this chapter with a challenge to think of multiple unique uses for a simple every day object. Here are some additional simple ways to incorporate creativity into your busy life and open your mind to the possibilities, even when you might only have a few minutes to spare:

- Write down one problem you need ideas for at the top of a page. Set a timer and take a ten minute break from whatever work you are involved in. Then write all the ideas that come to mind as you focus on just that one problem.

- Listen to music without lyrics for five minutes. Let your mind wander, jotting down any thoughts that arise.

- Write down three problems at the beginning of the day and keep the short list in plain sight. As you go through your day, jot down any thoughts that come to you regarding those three specific problems.

▸ Ask a friend, colleague, or family member what ideas they
might have about an issue that is puzzling you. Listen
with an open mind to what they come up with. To expand
the thinking, ask someone who isn't involved in or familiar
with the concept. Corporate coaches that don't have experience with your particular area of work are sometimes
the best; they have an outside view looking in instead of a
biased view.

▸ Attend an organizational meeting of a group you don't
typically associate with (for example, if you are an engineer, go to a writer's club meeting). I attend a variety of
business organization meetings, attracted to them based
on the topic. I've heard from oil and gas executives, human
resource personnel, engineers, marketing gurus, coaches
and dreamers. I find it thought provoking, inspiring and
motivating to spice up my life with the variety of information and perspectives. Hanging out with a different crowd
can inspire new ways of thinking and ideas. It may be the
hardest challenge on this list for some people to do, and it
does take a bit more time than those just mentioned, but
trust me — it's definitely worth trying!

If you have more time and can get a group of people together
to work on creative problem solving, consider these more formal
ways to get new ideas and perspectives on issues that have been
stalled or hit a roadblock by playing off the ideas of others.

Here is a simple way to "pass around the problem" and collect
varying input: Invite everyone in a group to take a sheet of paper

and write down a problem they are having at work, providing enough information so that a person reading it would understand the issue. It could be something specific from work that was giving them a headache or work in general. Maybe they are looking for a solution or another way to approach a situation; maybe they want more responsibility so that they can eventually earn a promotion, but aren't sure how to ask for it. The issues can be just about anything.

Once everyone's problem has been clarified, everyone passes their problem one person to the right. Everyone takes one minute to read their neighbor's problem and write down their advice, reactions, ideas, direction, empathy, ask questions, offer suggestions and assistance, or respond in any way they are able to. After one minute, the problem gets passed to the person to the right and the process continues until each person has their original problem back in their hands, now with multiple solutions suggested.

The point of the exercise is to move people out of their comfortable thinking ruts, and allow them to examine their problems from a different perspective. It really helps to get a fresh perspective on your problems when you've been wrapped up in them for a while. Try this at your next work meeting, or over dinner with your family or friends. I've used this exercise in both places with great results.

A second method to spark creativity, open up your mind to other perspectives, and lift you out of ruts is through the use of random word generators. First, have your group define a problem. Then choose a random word for discussion. As a group, try to connect the random word to the problem and come up with possible solutions. It may or may not lead to a brainstorm of thoughts. If not, choose another random word, and focus on it to see where the discussion leads. Record your ideas and investigate practical possibilities further. Random words can be produced a number of ways, including from thin air, from books with tables of random words, or by using a chart (see the sample chart a little later in this chapter). You can use this technique on your own, by creating a random word chart and playing with the words in reference to a selected problem, to see if you can create other possibilities than what you were previously considering.

How would random word generation work in a practical application? I always liked this story.

 A group was trying to solve the problem of ice forming on power lines in the northern states. They used random-word charts to solve the problem. They were sent out on the meeting's hotel grounds to pick up objects from anywhere they walked and bring them back to the room. One man purchased a jar of honey in the gift shop. When everyone returned to the meeting room, the group was instructed to fill out the left hand column of an empty chart with the names of the objects they'd retrieved. Then they were to work across the chart, filling in the

first word or phrase that came to their mind when they thought of the object, proceeding down each word in the column and writing random words across the rows.

The group used the words in everyone's charts as conversation starters to try to solve the ice problem. The gentleman who'd bought the honey had "bear" and "sugar" among the random words in his chart. He started the conversation by suggesting they put honey pots at the top of the power poles to attract bears that would then climb the poles to get the honey. The bears climbing the poles would cause them to vibrate and knock the ice off the wires.

As impractical as that is, the idea inspired them to think about vibration, and that is how they eventually solved the problem: they flew helicopters over the lines to cause the lines to sway and the ice fell off. Today there are devices on the poles to shake the lines to keep ice from forming or heat to melt the ice.

So, I invite you to have some faith and hope in this methodology. You never know where it might lead. Use this example chart to get your ideas flowing.

RANDOM WORDS CREATIVITY EXERCISE

For each word in the left-hand column, write down the first word or phrase that comes to mind, one in each box going across until the chart is filled. I filled in the chart below with my random words and phrases as an example.

Random Words	Associated Words/Phrases		
bridge	Mackinac Island	engineer	connect
golf ball	ditch	competition	pink
pocket	suit	secret	trinkets
bread	oven	home-made	butter
envelope	check	love letter	bills

Create your own random word chart. Use the phrases and words in your chart to create possibilities and alternative options for a problem you are dealing with.

1. Decide on a problem or issue — personal or professional — that you would like to experiment with.

2. Fill in the first column of the chart below with objects you see in the room you are in.

Random Words	Associated Words/Phrases		

4. Spend a few minutes filling in the rest of the chart moving across each row, with words or phrases the word in the first column makes you think of.

5. Play with the words in your completed chart, considering the problem you want to solve, and see what ideas come up for you as you think about different random words.

Another creative idea-inspiring method that you can use either on your own or with a group is the use of questions.

"What if...?" It's a simple question — with endless possibilities for answers. The use of this question can open up so many opportunities for you.

 In a training class I attended on creativity, the instructor posted several flipchart pages on the walls with one question at the top of each chart. We were instructed to move up to the flipcharts in pairs, armed with a single magic marker, and to take turns responding to the question without talking.

We spent a few minutes with our partner on one chart and then moved to the next chart and question. We developed a writing rhythm and silent signals to let our partner know we wanted to write. It was an interesting exercise.

The question that intrigued me the most was "What if there were 48 hours in a day?" Wow, that really got me thinking. What if there were? I would certainly spend about ten of them sleeping without any guilty feelings. There would be time for everything including time to just sit there and do nothing more than enjoy the beauty of the world around me. To have twice as much time as we have now. In the words of Dr. Seuss "Oh, the Places You'll Go!"

When we were instructed to write our own "What If," I wrote "What If Everyone Enjoyed Their Work?" and it got me thinking. What would happen if we did? Well, it might seem weird at first, right? But then imagine what great things would happen with productivity, working relationships, creativity and innovation. Mondays would be the happiest day of the week. Everyone would be in the right place doing the work they do the best. That got me thinking about how we could really make that happen. It started a very creative idea chain reaction.

What will you do with this "What If" exercise? Use it for your own self-discovery? Share it with friends? What "What If?" would you post in the lunchroom, on the agenda for your next meeting, or at home for your family members to consider? What do you think would happen if you opened up the thinking process of your coworkers or family with that simple question?

Think about your SOS to WOW challenge. Right now you are stuck in the Same Old Stuff. What if things were different? Suppose you are working on health and fitness and don't think exercise is fun. A "What If?" might be "What if all exercise was fun?" Then what? If advancing in your career is your SOS, a "What If?" might be "What if I knew there were no limitations to my advancement in this company?" If that were the case, how would you act differently?

What is a "What If?" question you could apply to your SOS to WOW journey right now? Write it here.

Now brainstorm a list of all the things that come to mind when you consider the "What If?" to be true.

1

2

3

4

5

Refer back to this list and add to it throughout your journey, and see what comes up for you.

Experiment with other questions. Share your "What If" questions with others to see what additional ideas are sparked beyond your personal list. I also encourage you to try some of your "What Ifs." It may take some time to get used to your new way of being (now might be a good time to read, or re-read, Chapter 5 of this book, Getting Your Mojo to Flow). While there are bound to be setbacks, once you see the benefits of the change, you will be motivated to plow forward. Apply it to your own personal SOS to WOW journey.

Another creativity-inspiring exercise is my "One Question" technique.

To boost your creativity factor, write down one question each day that you would like answered and think about it throughout the day. You don't have to problem-solve the question, just keep it in mind and be open to any ideas that might come up. The question can be about anything. It may be how to fix a problem, how to handle a difficult person, or how to make a decision you are contemplating. I've tried the experiment myself and found that when I spend a few minutes focusing on the question first thing in the morning and then let it go, answers came to me throughout the day when my brain was relaxed—for example when I was driving to a place I've been to many times before or when exercising.

The key is to pose the question and write it down or remember it in some other way, so that you can occasionally refer to it throughout the day. Be open to the possibility that the answer may come to you in some unsuspecting way. Someone may say something or do something that gives you an idea. You may read something in a magazine or online, or hear something on the radio that sparks an inspiration. Be open to insights coming from anywhere, as well as to the possibility that nothing may come to you that day. If that happens, save the question to repeat on another day. Don't give up on finding an answer. What question will you play with tomorrow?

CHANNEL YOUR INNER CHILD

When we are children our creativity is free and flowing. The older we get though, the more rules and procedures we are required to follow, and the less likely we are to veer from the beaten path. I've presented on careers at schools from elementary grade levels though high school and college. I've blended my presentation to include engineering, training, executive coaching and fitness. One of the most results-producing and fun exercises I've made a part of my presentation games is the paper airplane game. It is a game that connects to all of my "careers," combining fitness (the wild building, throwing and running to retrieve planes that don't make it into the landing zone), creativity (playing with ideas on how), engineering (the process of making the planes and figuring out how to get them in the landing area), coaching (managing and working with a team, and encouraging and acknowledging team successes) and training (using the game to illustrate a key learning point). The point is to get participants to think outside of the box, and open up their creative thinking while enjoying a fun game with a little competitive spirit mixed in.

Groups are divided into teams of four or five players with each team given a stack of different colored paper. A starting line and a landing zone are marked on the floor with masking tape. The team players are not allowed to cross over the starting line when launching their airplanes. Only planes that are completely in the landing zone count, and the goal is to be the team with the most paper airplanes in the landing zone at the end of the time.

Teams are given two minutes to play the game. With very min-imal rules provided at the start of the game, teams start making assumptions about what they can and cannot do. I try not to give the teams any strategy time because then they start asking ques-tions, and I don't want to give away the game by shrugging my shoulders at each question.

Many different learning points emerge in the game. Perhaps the most important one is that we focus on rules. Even though there are few rules in the game, participants always make assumptions and this hinders our creative thinking. I intentionally provide just a few rules and don't answer any questions the teams have regarding what a plane is supposed to look like to prevent restrictive thinking.

The first time I played this game, my inclination was to pick up the entire pack of paper and throw it into the landing zone. But I told myself it was the paper airplane game and we had to fold planes before throwing, so I proceeded to fold planes. Then a minute later another team picked up their entire pack of paper and threw it over the line to win. I was appalled they'd "stolen" my idea! Of course, they really hadn't; I was just upset with myself for talking myself out a great idea. It's amazing how creative peo-ple can get with this game. I once had some teams run out and pick up the planes that didn't make it into the landing zone and re-fly them (remember, I only said they couldn't cross the line when launching). And, I've only once had a participant claim the others were cheating, (which they weren't), because they didn't actually fold "real" paper airplanes.

So, what lessons typically come out of the airplane game?

1. You may think you aren't creative, but when it comes down to it, you can really come up with some interesting ideas — especially under the pressure of a two-minute game time clock.

2. The assumptions you make can control and restrict your actions.

3. Following rules too strictly can prevent you from testing boundaries.

4. Sometimes we take ourselves too seriously (like the fellow who was adamant about what qualified as a plane).

5. People tend to be risk avoiders and instead tend to not try creative ideas they think might not be allowed (for example my not throwing the whole pack of paper because it might not be ok).

6. Sticking with the way you've always done things and not being open to new ways of approaching projects and processes can hold you back.

7. Once judgments are made, people tend to stick with their first idea or opinion and close themselves off to other possibilities.

IT'S OK, EVEN GOOD SOMETIMES, TO COLOR OUTSIDE OF THE LINES

In order to remind adults to "color outside of the lines" and think outside the proverbial box, I like to utilize creativity exercises in my speaking engagements and training classes.

When training, I always have a backup creativity exercise ready in case some of the participants have already been exposed to my planned game in a previous presentation. I prepare quart size plastic bags for each small group and fill the bags with a half dozen items (the same ones in each bag). I've included props like a bag of M&Ms, a die, and a pipe cleaner. Each group gets a bag and is instructed to create a word related to the training topic using the first letter of each item they were given. Most people will play with the items in the bag but almost no one thinks to use the bag itself as one of the items. What would you have done? I invite you to look at things from all angles, so as not to miss an opportunity. Remember, it's not "all in the bag!"

This chapter has provided you with a multitude of ideas for boosting creativity. Obviously you can't try them all at once, and some will work better for you one day (or for one situation) than another. Remember that taking time to play with creativity and develop new ideas will resolve many problems. Keep coming back here as you travel the path from SOS to WOW.

FEARLESS FORWARD MOVEMENT

RISK TAKING

Risk is inevitable. It is part of everyday life. Every time we walk out of the house, we are taking a risk with the air we breathe (more so in some places than others). When we ride the bus or carpool or even drive ourselves, we are taking a risk to some degree with our safety and our lives on the roads. Even picking a partner for life is risky; how much do two people really know about one another when they say "I do"? Not to be overly pessimistic, but even folks who eat healthy and exercise can still get sick or die from an unforeseen illness. The point is, risk is everywhere and we can't avoid it. We do what we can to mitigate our risks, but risks are part of life, and they must be faced.

Risk taking is the process of taking action, (or sometimes, even no action), when you aren't sure what the outcome will be.

Remember, nothing is guaranteed. You are always exposing yourself to the possibility of losing something or gaining something along the way.

To move from SOS to WOW involves taking risks at some point or many points along the way. The change you are working toward may seem huge to you, but to others it may not be that way. We all have a different perception of what risk is.

To some, jumping out of an airplane is a high risk, while for others it is just another exciting adventure they packed into a fun filled weekend. Moving to a new city or country may terrify some people, while others would be excited to have the opportunity to see the world. I've conducted a survey in my business classes on risk taking and asked them to answer by show of hands how they felt about certain situations ranging from placing a $100 bet at a blackjack table in Vegas to speaking in public. I asked them to answer low, medium, or high to each. The answers were all over the place. There wasn't a single person who consistently answered all low, all medium or all high for all situations, or one situation that everyone classified at a certain level of risk. We have perceptions of risk based on experiences we've had in our past. We've been successful and not so successful in our undertakings, and the results all leave their imprint in our minds.

When I graduated from college, (Michigan State University), I was determined to find work in a warmer climate near the water. An engineering degree afforded me opportunities all across the country, and I settled on Houston, Texas. When I interviewed in the month of December it was 70 degrees without a cloud in the sky and I decided that is where I wanted to be. I thought moving to a new state and starting a new job would be a grand time, though I had some apprehension in moving so far away from home.

I was talking to a girlfriend from high school before I headed south and she told me I was so brave. I had no idea why she said that at the time because to me it was the next natural step after college and moving south was going to be fun. That was before I arrived in Houston during Rodeo week, when everyone was wearing Western gear and trail riders were coming into town on horses and I wondered if it was always like that here ... and before I was stuck in a hotel for weeks before my belongings arrived in a town where I didn't know a soul.

Once I was in my apartment and settled, things became quite a bit easier but there were still many teary-eyed telephone calls home to mom and dad before that feeling subsided.

Though a bit rough in the beginning, my move turned out to be a very successful risk. For me, ignorance was bliss (regarding how brave I was really going to have to be to make it through those tough months). But ignorant or not, I highly recommend taking calculated risks in your life. For example, it would have been much more of a risk if I had just packed up and moved without having a job in the new town. I know several people who have done just that and they are doing quite well. But I'm not sure I would have taken that big of a risk. As I mentioned earlier, the perception of what is a small or big risk is different for every one of us.

Think about some of the risks you have taken in your life. Does one successful one stand out among the others? It may be hard to pick out a "successful" risk because, to you, it may not have seemed like a risk when you were doing it. Just like my move from Michigan to Texas. My girlfriend thought I was being brave, but at the time I made the decision, I didn't think about it that way. It wasn't until I was in the middle of the experience that the riskiness of the situation became clear to me. That may be true for you too.

Here's an example of successful risk taking. I attended a business meeting on change in the energy industry, and our table ice breaker topic before the speaker presented was to discuss a change we made that was successful. I was intrigued by the story my tablemate shared on some major risks she had undertaken. She started out as a teacher in a safe stable position, as she described it, but really wanted real growth in her career. Through a series of positives and negatives including pay cuts, career restarts, skillful negotiations, additional higher education, and the death of close family members, she was able to accomplish that goal. While she was sometimes sidetracked by an underlying fear of failure and the fear of making the same mistakes she had seen others make when they started their own business, she managed to come out on top. How did she do it?

▸ She didn't let herself be susceptible to the stress and fears that could have dragged her down.

▸ She performed an internal review of herself and knew she had what it took to make it on her own.

▸ She learned new critical skills by researching, listening to, and watching those she worked with, and then practiced doing what made them successful.

▸ She used the comment that "you'll be back" from a boss at the company she left as a strong motivator to jump on the opportunity to excel.

▸ She took calculated (not blind) risks, understanding her own strengths and weaknesses.

▸ She loosened her grip on her plan and stepped out on "a leap of faith."

▸ She appreciated that she wasn't the only one risking something — at times others were taking a risk on her.

There are many great tips from her experience to apply in our own lives to take and make more successful risks. Which one resonates with you? How might you apply it to your own journey?

Spend some time thinking about successful risks
you have taken. You may not have had as many
standout ones as my tablemate, but I'll bet that
the longer you think about it, the more successes
you will be able to come up with.

* Which one was most significant for you?

* What did you learn from it?

WHAT ABOUT THE FAILURES?

It seems easier to recall the times we have messed up than it is to acknowledge when we did things right, doesn't it? That's because we are hard on ourselves! We tend to focus on what goes wrong.

I recall being invited to speak to a crowd of people at a local conference many years ago when I was a young presenter. The predicted attendance guesstimated by the conference organizer was that it might be 150-200. I'd spoken to groups of 100-200 before with great success. This time the topic — on dealing with egos, personalities and politics — drew a record crowd of close to 400 people. The event went well, but there was some distraction and confusion scattered about the audience during my presenta-tion because some of the interactions and exercises I presented would have worked better with a smaller crowd.

Was it a disaster? Not at all. A learning opportunity? Definitely. The majority of the feedback I received was positive, with only a few comments about what could have worked better. But you notice, *I still refer to that experience as a failure.* On the upside, sometimes failures are just what we need. They become great learning experiences. I've since had the opportunity to work with crowds of that size or larger many times, and have attended workshops and researched tips and techniques for handling them that work very well for me. I even teach workshops on speaking and training and have real life examples of techniques I can share with attendees that have produced success for me. Sometimes we don't even know what we don't know, so we will be surprised at times, but will make it through just fine. Maybe I'll have the pleasure of having you in my audience someday — at a conference or one-on-one.

Think of a risk you've taken that resulted in some type of failure. Remember, a risk isn't always something planned. Taking action (or inaction) when you are not sure how things will turn out is taking risk. Taking on the large group for me is an example of one.

* Write down your unsuccessful risk.

* What did you learn from it?

* What will you do with that knowledge?

PUT THE PAST IN THE PAST

Unsuccessful risks can hold us back because we hold onto our stories from the past throughout our lives. These stories lead to our assumptions about not being able to succeed (see Chapter 7 for more about assumptions), which lead us to inaction and keep us in SOS. How can you get past the failures and move on to taking chances again?

The solution is pretty simple: *just do it*. After my presentation to a large group that didn't go as well as I had hoped, did I stop speaking? No. I went right on to the next presentation, this time armed with new knowledge and determined to improve. I know what you are thinking. "Just do it" is much easier said than done. It isn't always easy to pick yourself back up and jump back in. Give yourself a reasonable amount of time to reflect on what happened without self blame. Consider what you learned from your experience and how will you move forward with that information. Relate your lesson learned to future opportunities where you can apply it, and commit to trying it next time, making a plan to incorporate it in your actions. Remember Isaac Newton's First Law of Motion: "An object at rest tends to stay at rest, unless acted upon by an external force." Once you give yourself a little push over the first hurdle, the path will get easier, I promise.

It is also important to look at your assumptions (as Chapter 7 addresses) and consider how those hold you back. How many times have you let an unexpected result deter you from trying something new? A few years ago, my friends and I attended a live fashion show in Houston and had some amazing experiences by *not* letting our assumptions get in the way.

Fashion Week in Houston had been around for a few years, but my friends and I had just discovered it. The event takes place at the Wortham Center in the downtown theatre district and features over sixteen designers over the course of four nights, including several from Houston. The night we attended, my girlfriends and I arrived soon after the doors opened to make sure we wouldn't miss a thing. The front entrance to the Wortham was an official red carpet complete with "pretend paparazzi" surrounding us to take our pictures.

Once inside, we located our seats and then were off exploring what there was to see and do. We happened to wander into the Green Room, (where celebrities are interviewed and performers can relax). You might assume you could only get in there with some kind of pass or invitation, but we didn't let assumptions deter us and walked right in. We did not encounter any resistance, and the Green Room became our break room throughout the event, a place where we could people watch and enjoy a few free cocktails.

At the end of the evening we were invited by the announcer to attend the after party, with dancing models

and thumping pumping music. We decided the action inside was not worth the additional $20 cover charge at
the door, and headed back to our Green Room to relax
and recharge.

It was there I met a VIP member of the press in the ladies room. She mentioned that in addition to the fashion
event, there were fabulous affairs happening all over
town, and she gave me her business card to connect with
her if we were interested. I exited the powder room and
met up with my friends, sharing my delight at having
a new adventure-seeking partner. They teasingly dared
me to ask her if she had passes for the after party, as
many members of the press would. Not being one who
can resist a dare, I returned to the restroom and found
my new friend there still working on her hair. And, since
I don't enjoy begging people for anything, I turned my
friends' dare into a playful question.

I asked the newswoman "Do you happen to know any
secret passageways into the after party?" To my surprise her reply was "as a matter of fact I do, follow me."
And I did, but not before grabbing my friends from the
Green Room. Holding hands we followed our fearless
leader along a pitch black hallway, carefully edging our
way up the dark stairway into the party. We passed a
police officer who gave us a nod and a grin when he
saw our leader. To our delight, in less than a minute, we
were right in the middle of the action. We bid a brief

good-bye to our new friend, checked out the party for a short while, and headed out into the late evening to our car, totally exhilarated from our fashion adventure.

The moral of the story? It never hurts to ask. You just might find yourself being led up a dark stairway into an adventure you would have otherwise missed!

So, maybe you've asked a question before and received a no. Maybe you've tried something and it didn't work. Maybe your painful memories hold you back from trying the same things again. I encourage you to look for ways to try again. Hopefully you've already found some within the pages of this book.

Need more inspiration? Do an Internet search on "famous failures," and you will find countless examples of people who were unsuccessful at an attempt but got back up and tried again, sometimes many times, before they achieved their dream.

Michael Jordan, the famous basketball player, was cut from his high school basketball team. Albert Einstein's teachers said he would never amount to much. Oprah Winfrey was demoted from her news anchor position because the news station claimed she wasn't fit for television. Meryl Streep was told she was too ugly for a part in a movie when she was young. Her reply? "You are only one opinion in a sea of thousands and I am off to find a kinder tide." These people didn't let being turned down stop them. Don't let anyone tell you what you can or cannot do. Believe in yourself — you know you the best.

* What previous unsuccessful risk is still holding you back?

* What will you do to gain the courage to get back up and try again?

Fear can stop us from acting, and not taking action may lead to regret.

Years ago, I stayed at a Jamaican resort where the nightly entertainment included a group of circus performers who, during the day, let guests try the trapeze with the performers as their guides. I decided to try it, and after a terrifying first step off the platform, I spent much of that vacation flipping and getting caught by the other performer, and landing safely in the net. Years later, I discovered a trapeze training facility in Austin and my girlfriend (the only one brave enough, or maybe crazy enough, to join me) and I headed west to "join the circus."

We arrived at the trapeze school, signed our life away, and proceeded to gear up, getting wrapped and clipped and cinched to uncomfortable levels. Then, it was time to climb. Compared with my Jamaican hotel experience, the trapeze seemed so much higher. The climb up the tiny ladder to the platform 30 feet in the air seemed so much scarier. Once at the top, the assistant unclipped me from one cable for my safe climb up the ladder, and onto the other cable for safety on the platform.

"Hold on to that pole," she said, "so that I can get you clipped." I hugged the pole like my life depended on it; it really did! Finally, it was time for me to fly. I was told to step to the edge of the platform and place all ten toes over the edge. But my body wouldn't move forward. Frozen at the thought of really doing it, I reminded myself that others waited below me for their turn, and that finally propelled me to the edge of the platform. I was clipped and strapped and there was a net, and there wasn't any reason to fear for my life — right?

But I did fear for my life. Still, I reached out and grabbed the trapeze, and the assistant held me while I leaned forward like Rose DeWitt Butaker in the movie *Titanic* when she and Jack Dawson were hanging out at the front of the ship before the accident. I waited for the cue from the instructor on the ground, "Hep," meaning jump. And I did jump, screaming all the way. And it was incredibly awesome.

Even though we prepare to take a risk, build up our courage and do all the research, and even when we've done it before, it can still be a scary to take the jump. The same feelings that arise when you are about to take a physical risk can come up when we take a personal risk. Whether you are about to change your career, or tell someone what you really think, or make a change to something that has worked for years, it is not uncommon for feelings of anxiety, tightness in the chest, rapid heartbeat and shaking to occur.

Not taking action, can also produce those feelings. My circus adventure friend hesitated every time the trapeze flyers said "Hep," and for almost the entire day, each time, she climbed back down the ladder, defeated. Finally, near the end of our flying time, she convinced herself to jump ... and she loved every minute of it. On our drive home, she was upset with herself for hesitating on all of the previous attempts and missing out on more flying time.

TAKE THE FIRST STEP

So often, the first step is the hardest to take: the first day of a diet; the first time we speak in public; the first time we create something and put it out there for reactions; the first step off the trapeze platform. Don't regret the things you didn't say or didn't try. Take a chance and enjoy the flight! The more steps you take, the easier it gets. Don't be afraid of that first step. Trust in yourself. It will be so much more fun than you ever imagined. Just Jump!

Make a list of five fears that are keeping you from WOW.

1

2

3

4

5

Analyze each fear by first asking yourself if it is real. What negative outcome do you expect or worry about? What can you do to prevent or adjust the negative outcome? (For example, suppose your WOW goal is to find a new job. Some of the things you might be afraid of are not being able to find another job or your current boss firing you when he/she finds out you were looking for something else. Chances are you would be able to find another job, though maybe not as fast as you would like. It's also possible your boss would wish you well and be supportive of you.)

What if the fear that's holding you back isn't even true? How would that change how you act moving forward?

Consider each fear. Is it real? Is it true? What if the opposite were true? What would you do? Like the busted myths in Chapter 7, these are stories we tell ourselves.

Fear #1

Fear #2

Fear #3

Fear #4

Fear #5

When you identify and consider the possibilities associated with your fears, it is easier to move past them. Try it. More often than not, doing something, even though it scares you, really isn't going to be as bad as you think. You might even have a really good time.

Remember that traveling from SOS to WOW is a very personal journey and it may take you more or less time and more or less courage than others take for movement to occur. In propelling your movement from SOS to WOW, taking risks challenges your personal growth. Some examples of personal growth include speaking up, changing the process, and following through with ideas that aren't popular where you didn't follow through before.

You have to be courageous in order to move forward in your personal or professional life. Taking well-thought-out risks that apply directly to your WOW will lead to your growth in three potential areas: self-improvement, commitment and self-disclosure. (Note that risks don't always take a great deal of analysis; sometimes you can go through the process in ten seconds or less and have a successful outcome.)

What are these personal growth risks?

Self-improvement risk includes activities like learning a new language or other skill, taking on a difficult project at work to get ahead, starting a business, or making a move to another state. I once had a risk taking class participant who was afraid to learn a new language because she didn't want the responsibility that went along with it. She was afraid to gain the skill because she thought management would overwhelm her with work involving translations and other second language work. Fear of success can hold us back.

A second form of personal growth risk is **commitment risk**. This is committing to a cause, a plan, a person, a company or yourself on your journey from SOS to WOW. My husband and I regularly volunteer to dog-sit when my son and his fiancée go out of down. The dog is a sweetie and great fun. My husband teaches her tricks and spoils her with eggs for breakfast every morning. She follows him everywhere, sits in his lap when he works from home, and sleeps under the covers with him. We take her for walks in the park and enjoy every moment with her. The excitement that dog expresses when we come home is joyful. But, we don't want a dog full time. Always having an animal to take care of and the risk of not being able to find a reasonably-priced sitter when we travel are some of the reasons we opt out of that commitment. This is what I am referring to when I mention commitment — to a person (or animal!), cause or company. It's important to assess your own situations and decide how far you want to take your commitment, and what risks you will take.

The third category in personal growth is **self-disclosure risk**. It is expressing your inner thoughts to others typically by speaking up or out through conversations, writing or presenting. I've been writing since I was a little kid. I even made my own books with handmade cloth book covers in grade school. As we all have, I continued to write in school as well as at work — anything from memos (that is what they were called way back then before email!) to proposals and reports. I was once rehired by an executive based solely on my client meeting reports when our organization was reorganizing and the use of contractors (which I was), was being reevaluated. But when I first started non-work related writing, I hesitated and played with different book ideas for years. I wondered if people would be interested and think they were worthwhile. I finally took a risk on a small scale, writing blogs and articles. The positive feedback I received gave me more confidence and now I am writing books — sharing my feelings and thoughts for all to see.

How do the three categories of self-improvement, commitment and self-disclosure apply to
your SOS to WOW journey?

What type of risk will it take to move you ahead?

There may be many risks you need to take to
get to WOW. For now, focus on just one — the
one you believe will make the greatest impact on
your progress. Clarify it here.

Use it to work through the steps that follow. You
can always go back through the book later and
apply the same tips to the other risks you need
to take.

FIVE STEPS TO FOLLOW

Now that you've got a better understanding of what I mean by risk taking, it's time to get going and make your vision happen. How will you do that?

Here are the key steps to more successful risk taking:

1. **Clarify the risk taking goal.** What is it that you really want to do and what will it accomplish? How will it contribute to your journey to WOW?

2. **Brainstorm different ways you could accomplish the goal.** Be creative. Experiment with some of the exercises in Chapter 8 on creativity.

3. **Consider your risk taking tendencies.** Stretch yourself beyond your normal tendencies, but not too far outside your comfort zone (unless you are ready for that).

4. **Improve your chances of a successful risk outcome.** Some options include developing a prototype and test, sharing the risk with another person, or asking for or simply taking more time to collect information.

5. **Take action.** Just do it!

Let's examine each step in more detail.

#1 — CLARIFY THE RISK TAKING GOAL

First, get clear on the risk you want to take and your underlying goal. What is it that you really want? What change would you like to see and what needs to happen in order for that change to become a reality? You may have more than one desired change, but for now, just concentrate on one. (If you're working through this book as you go, you just did this step in the last exercise I gave.) Clarify your risk taking goal and what you will accomplish by taking the risk. Look back at your WOW goal from Chapter 2 and revisit the Heart 'n Smart concepts in chapter 4 to assist you in this process. Be specific. Instead of saying "I want to speak up more," clarify what you mean. For example, "I want to speak up in meetings where I've previously been silent and have my ideas heard, respected and acted upon." Then add the Heart part: "When I am able to do this, I will feel confident and be more respected in the workplace."

Write out one risk taking goal that will carry you forward on the path from SOS to WOW.

#2 — BRAINSTORM DIFFERENT WAYS TO ACCOMPLISH THE GOAL

There are many ways to accomplish any of our risk taking goals. If, for example, your goal is to find a new job, you could do some or all of the following:

▸ Quit your job; tell your boss today you are quitting and then start your search.

▸ Attend school at night to obtain a certification or degree to make yourself more marketable.

▸ Connect with a head hunter to engage their services.

▸ Network, both inside and outside your organization.

▸ Look within your current organization for posted positions you qualify for.

▸ Engage actively in social media to let people know you are looking.

▸ Connect with past schools/universities for connections and job boards.

▸ Connect with organizations related to your desired job; find ones that actively support job seekers by posting positions on their web sites or announcing open positions in their formal meetings.

Remember there is always more than one path to your goal. Utilize exercises like the random word generator detailed in Chapter 8 on creativity to come up with new ideas, and stay open to the possibilities.

#3 — CONSIDER YOUR RISK TAKING TENDENCIES AND EVALUATE ALTERNATIVES ACCORDINGLY

How do you know what your risk taking tendencies are? You probably have a pretty good idea based on the way you typically behave. Are you the one to jump out there and try something new or are you more cautious? As I discussed in Chapter 3, there are simple assessments you can take to determine your tendencies. If you search on the Internet you can find a number of free assessments to give you a fairly accurate reading. Those with a higher level of sophistication and accuracy are usually available through professional coaches focusing on creativity and risk, like myself. If that interests you, email me at margaret@ideasandbeyond.com.

In classes and presentations, I like to utilize a game from my childhood that offers an interesting perspective and opens up conversations on risk. It is called Red Light, Green Light, a sidewalk game I played as a child with my neighbors, and one you too may know. The object of the game is to be the first player to get to the person who is "it." The caller stands at the end of the sidewalk, facing away from the players, who gather some distance away. When the caller shouts out green light, the players move toward the caller at any pace. When the caller shouts out red light, the players must stop moving. The caller turns around to check to see if anyone is moving and sends the person back to start if they are. The first player to reach the caller is the winner and becomes the new caller.

I like to observe, and discuss with my participants the manner in which different players move toward the caller during the game as an indication of people's risk-taking tendencies. Some are cautious and take baby steps throughout the game. They may be that way in their daily lives, operating with a tendency to be overly cautious. Others run like a bat out of hell the entire game. These cautious or bat-out-of-hell risk takers tend to stay low or high on risk all the time. No matter what the situation, they are hiding in the back or are way, way out there taking chances with everything.

Then we have the creative risk takers. They may be high or low risk takers but they access each situation and make a choice based on the information they collect. So occasionally a high creative risk taker may not take a risk or act overly cautious, but over time their risk taking still averages high. And occasionally a low creative risk taker may really go all out there, but over time their risk taking still averages low.

And last you have the people that don't even step up to the plate to play. It may be for any number of reasons; maybe they are tired or have high heels on and are being safe or aren't comfortable yet with what I might ask them to do. I often experiment with scenarios including varying the penalties and prizes to delve deeper into risk tendencies. It is all quite interesting and serves as an entertaining risk model.

What kind of Red Light, Green Light player would you be?

Over the next several days, pay attention to your behavior in a number of different situations. What kind of a risk taker are you? Take note of your style and write some comments regarding why you think you are that way.

* I am a _____ (high, low, medium — addicted or creative) risk taker.

* I believe this to be true because:

* In what scenarios have your risk taking tendencies benefitted you?

* In what scenarios have your risk taking tendencies hindered you?

* What will you change?

You're undoubtedly familiar with the childhood story of Goldilocks and the three bears, but here's a reminder.

A little girl, Goldilocks, named for her beautiful blonde curly hair, went for a walk in the woods and came upon the house of a family of bears. She knocked, but no one answered so she went in. Tired and hungry, she was delighted to discover porridge on the kitchen table, and chairs and beds for resting. She tried them all. Upon each encounter, she decided one was "too this" and another "too that." Each time, she selected the one that was just right for her. She ended up asleep in one of the beds when the bears arrived home from their walk in the woods. The story ends with Goldilocks waking up to see the bears, and then running screaming back into the woods never to return. The traditional moral of the story focused on respect for others' property. But the point of my story is that Goldilocks always knew just what she wanted.

I ask my clients to think this way all the time. That is the premise of professional coaching. One example is my coaching conversation with a CEO regarding connecting with potential clients and moving particular connections forward in the sales process. He was debating between the extremes of taking a high risk approach versus letting things happen. "One was too much and the other was too little," he exclaimed. Referring to the story of Goldilocks, I asked, "What would put you right in the middle — just right for you?" He laughed and found the perfect place from himself.

And, I direct my yoga students on the Goldilocks philosophy, too. "Take the pose to the place where you feel it, but not so much that you cross the line to feeling pain. If you are breathing through your mouth you are working too hard. If you can't feel a stretch, you're not working hard enough." They know what is right for them.

Think again about the level of risk taking you are comfortable with. What is your risk-taking goal? What would you have to do to push yourself just a little bit beyond your comfort zone to make that goal a reality? If we stay too comfortable and don't challenge ourselves we may never reach the place we want to be. If we push too hard we may end up exhausted, overwhelmed and quit too early. Find the place that is *just right* for you.

List some different ways you could accomplish your risk-taking goal. If you're having trouble, use the creativity exercises I detail in Chapter 8 to help you brainstorm ideas.

1

2

3

4

5

* Which ones fit best with your risk taking style, yet stretch you a little bit beyond your comfort zone and get you to "just right"?

* Which one are you willing to commit to right now?

* How will you accomplish this?

Another tool you can use to take more of the right risks is to ask yourself: "What's the worst thing that can happen?"

What are you afraid of? What are you really afraid of? If you take that risk that scares you, what is the worst thing that can happen? Here's an example:

 I have a girlfriend who works for a company that has an office in Paris. Visiting and possibly living in Paris was always a dream of hers. But instead of telling her boss that was her long term goal, she just made indirect comments and hinted at wanting to live in Paris. She never realized her dream because she didn't speak up. What would have happened if she had straight out asked to go to Paris? She might have been able to go. Or, the answer might have been no. How terrible is that?

The first step, when hesitation exists, is to determine the worst things that can happen. Make a list of those possibilities. Then, for each one, ask yourself the question, "if that happened, could I handle it?" If there is a possible negative outcome, how would or could you prevent it? Examining your risk in this way removes the worry and puts you in a place of taking action and mitigating the possible negative consequences.

Let's examine the risk of me speaking up to the corporate executives at my fitness instructor job. Then I will ask you to follow the same steps in analyzing your own personal situation.

What is the worst thing that could happen if I were to speak up to executive management about my ideas regarding the company's direction, my job, or other related concerns?

I might be ignored or they could claim my ideas as their own. I doubt that any consequence would be as serious as being fired.

How would I feel if that actually happened?

Upset at first that I wasn't listened to or given credit for my ideas but I would then be more determined to try a different approach to get them to hear me out or get credit for my ideas and be given the opportunity to be involved in the implementation.

Could I handle it if the worst thing actually happened?

Yes, definitely.

How could I lower the possibility of being ignored or having my ideas hijacked?

1. *Make sure I presented them to the right people*

2. *Test my ideas out on other people in the company before presenting them to executives for verification of their appeal*

3. *Present the ideas in a group setting*

4. *Find a supporter at a higher level within the organization to assist me in moving my ideas forward*

How about your own situation? Considering your risk:

* What is the worst thing(s) that can happen?

* How would you feel if those things actually happened?

* Could you handle it if the worst thing actually happened?

* How could you lower the possibility of those things happening or prevent it? What could you do?

#4 — IMPROVE YOUR CHANCES OF A SUCCESSFUL RISK OUTCOME

When it comes down to actually taking the risk, you can't succeed if you don't try. But, when trying, there are many things you can do to improve your odds.

You can **share the risk.** When we take a risk we don't typically think about taking someone along with us for the ride. Yet, sharing a risk is one of the best ways to improve your chances of success. For example, if your risk is speaking to your boss, consider gaining support from your co-workers and approaching management as a united front (but don't gang up on them). I mentioned this in my previous example.

A few years back I went skydiving with a girlfriend. She was recently divorced and wanted to experience the thrill of jumping out of a perfectly good airplane, but wasn't ready to do it alone. So she asked me along, and we jumped tandem (strapped to an instructor). There is no denying our chances of success were much greater taking the instructor along for the ride versus jumping on our own … at least the first time!

Whether it is jumping out of an airplane or telling the boss what you really think about a project or idea, sharing the risk with another person can improve the chances of a successful outcome in so many ways. Consider partnering with a buddy the next time you venture out on a risk. The adage about safety in numbers is a true one.

Test a prototype, if the situation allows, by creating a smaller version of the process or trying a conversation out on co-workers, family members or friends for their input before approaching the individual you really want to suggest something to. You'll feel more confident in yourself if you've already had a mini-success. And you'll also get the chance to play out the scenario and come up with more strategies for getting the results you want.

If you need it, **ask for more time to evaluate your options.** Sometimes we feel pressured to respond or act. If you allow yourself more time to access a situation, you will be able to move forward more effectively. You can also ask for advice from a trusted advisor to help you work through your decisions. But stay aware of over analysis, you don't want to get so caught up in preparing that you never accomplish the task.

#5 — TAKE ACTION

You've addressed your fears. Now it is time to take action to move toward your WOW, and access what needs to be modified.

When taking risks, sometimes the hardest parts are deciding where to start and actually taking the first step. Remember you can always modify, adjust, and change your mind and your plan. Almost nothing is forever, so don't let that first step paralyze you.

 A friend and I were reminiscing about college recently and our initial difficulty in picking a major with so many options available combined with our diverse interests

to complicate the matter. When we were in school we thought that we had to pick something that we were going to do for the rest of our lives. As we examined the options, nothing stood out as the one career we wanted to have forever. So, we tried a variety of majors ending up with so many extra credit hours in so many diverse areas, but finally found our place.

The lesson? Getting a degree in anything is a strong starting position and a wonderful accomplishment. Remember that your options are endless and as you grow, it will be easier to make that first choice. The key is to get started somewhere.

If you've ever had anything piling up on your desk, counter or in a closet, you can probably relate to this next story about taking action. It's like the risk you've always wanted to take — sitting there — a reminder every day of what needs to be done — but instead of taking action, you keep "walking by" and ignoring it.

 They were multiplying on the hangers and it needed to be done. I grabbed the whole rack of them, it must have been twenty at least, and pulled them out in one giant armful that I couldn't see over as I walked and dropped them in a pile on the bedroom floor. My jean collection now lay haphazardly on the floor and a whole section of open space existed in my closet. I'd taken that all important first step and my jeans weren't going back until I

went through every one of them and tried them on and made a decision.

With each pair of jeans there was a story and a great memory, like the pair I had my first horseback riding lesson in, (is that the day I became a real Texan?) and the ones that I truly wore until the material became baby soft and my knees punched through the material. So, it was hard to let go of them. But I separated them into piles; ones that I was sure needed to be thrown out or given away, ones that I wasn't sure about, and ones that I would keep. At least I was making progress. After a few hours, and some nice trips down memory lane, I finally had a bag of beloved jeans sitting in the garage to wait for a Goodwill delivery date.

By breaking down the challenge into smaller pieces (i.e. smaller piles) and tackling things piece by piece, I was able to break through and make some progress — and you will too. There are emotional obstacles to overcome, but they too fall. And when the end is finally realized, it feels great!

Here's to tackling a risk — bit by bit!

As you continue your journey from SOS to WOW, remember that taking action — or failing to do so — comes with the risk of two possible kinds of loss: the outcome may leave you worse off than before, making it is a tangible loss for you; or the outcome may be less favorable than it might have been and you've lost out on an opportunity.

People sometimes forget that there is as much risk in taking action as there is in not taking action. For example, how many times have you waited on yourself or others to make a decision? By not deciding, it has been decided. Risk is involved.

 My husband and I both happened to be working from home recently. We were taking a lunch break while playing one of our favorite card games, cribbage, in the front room. The window shutters were open and I could see clearly across the street. It was garbage pick-up day. To my surprise, our neighbors across the street had piled a bunch of toys atop the closed lid of their garbage can.

From where I sat, they looked like brand new toys, especially the giant plush bright orange and white four-foot Nemo on the top of the pile. I couldn't believe they would throw away good toys. As I've said before, I'm a fervent recycler. Toys, clothes and household items go to charity and cardboard, plastic and glass go to the recycle collection at the Ellington Air Force base nearby. Surely there was something wrong with these toys for them to be on the corner waiting for the garbage collector. My husband suggested they might have been chewed up by

a dog or worn out and we just couldn't see it from where we sat. So, I let it go for a while — but kept thinking about it throughout the morning.

Not much later, immersed in my work, I was interrupted by my husband telling me I had 30 seconds to decide. "Thirty seconds for what?" I called out. "The garbage truck is coming around the corner!" he replied, and I sprang to my feet. I rushed out the door and quickly headed to the edge of the curb, jumping up and down and waving to catch the attention of the truck driver before entering the street. Once I confirmed he saw me, I sprinted across the street to inspect Nemo.

He was in pristine condition: bright and white and not a tear or a spot on him. I picked him up and examined the other toys. They too were in perfect condition. I asked the garbage collector if he wanted them. He shook his head no, so I scooped them all up. With a joyful stride, and my treasures in tow, I headed back to my house. Now, all of the toys except Nemo have been donated to Goodwill; Nemo stays on display in my office, and occasionally in my presentations and at trade shows, as a reminder to act — a reminder to take risks.

When there is an opportunity or a risk to take, more often than not, we hesitate, and think things over and dwell on the possibilities. Considering the options and the consequences is a good thing. But have you ever noticed that in the end, you usually do what you were going to do anyway, before all the thinking and procrastinating? What are you waiting for?

Think about some risks where you hesitated to
make a decision.

* What were they?

* Did you ever decide?

* If not, did you miss out on something?

* What did you learn from this?

Risk taking can carry rewards and spark feelings of excitement. I have created a 21 Day Risk Challenge, (see the Appendix for details) and invite you to take it on. Turn to the Appendix now, decide if you are in, and if so, proceed full steam ahead. Remember that each risk can be taken, modified to fit your needs or rejected and replaced with another risk you feel is appropriate. Taking small risks will up your confidence in approaching larger risks. Get started building your confidence and don't let yourself get discouraged. You may need to circle back to your original goal to see what needs to change for greater success. It is a process that loops back to start in many cases. The journey from SOS to WOW is a never-ending process. That's why it is SOS to WOW (Well On the Way), not SOS to DONE!

THE VOICES IN YOUR HEAD

SELF TALK

My favorite voices-in-my-head joke is this: "I wake up every day planning to be productive and then a voice in my head says 'Haha good one!' and we laugh and laugh and take a nap."

Talking to oneself, whether silently or aloud is something most everyone does. I know, there's some stigma associated with it, but the truth is, the internal conversations we have with ourselves can really help us think through situations and make sense of things.

 Lombard Street in San Francisco is known for the one-way block on Russian Hill, where eight sharp turns are said to make it the most crooked street in the world. The famous street has been in scenes in many movies and is

part of a comedy sketch in which the comedian jokingly remarks that the flowers are planted for those people who killed themselves trying to drive down it.

I am fortunate to be able to spend time in the City by the Bay — a personal favorite — every year. Once, on vacation with my family, we rented an SUV for a day so that we could visit the Twin Peaks (hills near the center of San Francisco with a complete 360 degree view of the city), the redwoods in Muir Woods, and walk the Golden Gate Bridge. At the end of our adventurous day we headed back into the city toward our hotel and, as the driver, I found myself with a decision to make: either turn right and take the "safe" route to our hotel, or head up the back side of the famous Lombard Street and experience driving down those hairpin turns.

My husband, the front seat passenger, was gently advising "no, turn right" while my oldest son, the backseat driver, was nudging me to head straight up Lombard Street. I wasn't that comfortable driving the over-sized rental vehicle in a town where compact cars are the norm, and in the past I've always felt like my vehicle was going to flip over backwards when driving up steep grades. I'm pretty sure there aren't any documented cases of cars flipping over backwards driving up Lombard Street. If there were, it wouldn't still be there, right? So, in my head this conversation was going on, where I was talking myself into and out of heading up the hill. There was the excitement of trying something I'd never done before that was a little scary but at the same time, enticing; the fear of upsetting my husband who was cautiously advising me to take the safe route; and the strong desire to show courage and a bit of fun to my children. Ultimately, up and over won out.

I headed straight up the hill at the light instead of turning right. Adrenaline was pumping as I still wondered whether we would make it up without tipping over backwards. We did. And we made it down the front side of the crooked street winding slowly and steadily and safely. It was exciting, especially for the kids in the back seat, with mom at the wheel.

Talking to yourself can be a good thing. The caveat is that you have to do so constructively. Too often, we let assumptions and negative self-talk build up and create unfounded fears in our heads. You can't necessarily put a stop to those conversations going on in your head in the short term without a lot of focused practice over the long term. But, you can calm or quiet down the negativity and get focused on other things.

Meditation and focus exercises can assist you with quieting your mind. If you're struggling with negative self-talk, one suggestion is to turn back to and review Chapters 5 and 6.

As you use self talk to reach your WOW goal, it's important to have:

- ▸ **a conscious awareness of what is happening** — is there chatter in your head?

- ▸ **a reflection** — is the chatter negative, or positive and helpful?

- ▸ **a conscious effort to create a new pattern** — what are you trying to achieve?

Start by figuring out what you want *for you* instead of worrying about what others think. We are regularly bombarded with advice from books, magazines, and sometimes friends and family telling us what we should do in order to achieve a certain state of being that they believe we should achieve. Problems can arise when we only believe others, and follow their "should"s instead of listening to our hearts and our wants and our desires. "Don't let other people 'should' on you," I frequently advise my clients. Review your WOW destination to reinforce what you truly want for you. Remember the Goldilocks lesson from Chapter 9. You know what is *just right* for you. Pay attention to your intuition and trust yourself to follow through with it. You don't have to change your thoughts or behaviors when someone else makes a comment. Stick with what is truly you.

Looking for another way to work on maintaining the focus on what you want for you?

As I mentioned in Chapter 1, I am the 7th child of eight in a large Catholic family. I have five brothers and two sisters. When we went on family vacations, we always drove; ten airline tickets were cost prohibitive. Being on the road so much, we made up games and played well-known ones as well. One of our favorites was Punch Bug Slug Bug. That's where you keep your eye out for Volkswagen Beetle cars (or bugs), and when you spot one, you yell out "punch bug slug bug" and the color, and "gently" punch your brother or sister in the arm. It's great fun. And a great example of focusing attention. Once we started the game, we saw bugs everywhere. If we hadn't been playing the game, those same cars would still have driven by or sat in parking lots, they'd just have gone unnoticed.

My point? Once you set your attention on something, you can get ideas from everywhere if you are open to receiving them. If you're looking for them, you will see, hear, and experience things that previously passed right by. Decide to start your day open to solutions to a problem you need resolved, a question you want answered, or an area of your life you want ideas and options for. As you go about your day, you will probably be surprised how many ideas, thoughts and solutions come to you simply because you are now open to what you might not have been open to before.

An assessment that I use in coaching and training is the Creatrix,™ which measures your creativity and risk-taking orientations.

Creativity is the ability to produce new ideas and possibilities. Risk-taking is driving the idea forward, even in the face of adversity. Together they equal innovation. The results of the Creatrix provide you with tips on how to improve your creativity and risk taking to allow innovation to flow more easily. I work with clients — from professionals to executives — utilizing Creatrix results as a framework for personal and professional growth.

Growth requires pulling ideas out of our heads and developing the courage to implement them. The coaching process provides practical steps to open our creative minds, unleashes our ideas (we all have the answers within), and allows us to analyze and create actionable steps to take risk and make things happen.

One of the drivers for creativity, and part of the Creatrix model, is inner-directedness. Internally-directed people determine their own expectations and norms, and march to their own drummer. They don't let others "should" on them.

So what can you do to be more inner-directed and experience less "should-ing"?

For any situation, practice asking yourself "what would I really do, or want to do, in this situation? What am I really looking for?"

Here is an exercise to get your attention and self-talk focused on what *you* want. It is not so much about creating what does not exist in your world yet, though that can happen, but opening awareness to what you are missing that is already there.

Using your WOW vision as a springboard for positive ideas, write down all of the specific things you want to be, do and have when you reach WOW! For example - if you are trying to focus on health and fitness, here is a list of some things you might want:

<u>What I Really, Really Want:</u>

1. my jeans to be loose

2. my weight to go down

3. numerous healthy choices whenever I go out to eat

4. fun ways to exercise

5. the ability to stay on track with healthy eating habits

6. to feel fabulous

7. to be fabulous

8. to be able to do things I couldn't do before because of my weight

Some people find it easier to start with a list of all the things they don't want to have happen, (remember how we tend to focus on the negative), and then write the exact opposite of each to create their Do Want list. If that works better for you, give it a go. Just remember to erase or dispose of the Don't Want list as soon as you have your Do Want list created so that the negatives are out of your mind and only the positives remain in focus. Make a list of Really Do Wants (I call them really, really wants) for your SOS to WOW situation.

What I Really, Really Want:

1.

2.

3.

4.

5.

6.

7.

For at least the next 21 days every morning and every night, review the things you do want to happen with regard to your SOS to WOW journey. That is how long they say habits take to become natural for you (though for deeply ingrained limiting beliefs some psychologists say it can take six months or more), Either way, having patience and persistence is key. It doesn't matter if you sit in the hammock with a beer, or pray over the list, or place it by your bedside and read it at night before you go to sleep and first thing in the morning when you wake up. Do what works for you, just make sure you look at your "What I Really, Really Want" list at least twice a day, and spend some time reflecting on it. Be sure to focus on the feelings that being in the "really want" state will give you. Imagine yourself actually there. Then stay open to whatever ideas and opportunities come to you from wherever they might appear and see what happens. Like the Punch Bug Slug Bugs I talked about earlier, people and things that you missed when you were in a negative self-talk mode will be visible once you are focused on the positive. Try to resist thinking you need to do something to make everything on the list come true. Remember, this is a "want" list, not a "things to do" list.

How much do you really want your want? The key to success here is desire.

I was a Girl Scout when I was young and always enjoyed selling Girl Scout cookies. Knocking on doors to sell Girl Scout calendars was not the same delightful reaction you received when people opened the door and found out you were selling cookies. And I loved eating them too.

This latest cookie season the Girl Scouts came out with a new gluten free cookie. They were temptingly chock full of oatmeal and chocolate chips, and I was hooked after the first bite. But they were hard to find. Inevitably my skimpy supply was depleted and I craved that oatmeal and chocolate chip combination but could not find them anywhere.

One Sunday as I was headed to Galveston Island to host a yoga on the beach, I surprisingly missed my freeway exit on my very familiar beach route. I had to wind from the main street on the island through one-way streets and dead ends to get to the beach. Somehow I ended up right next to a grocery store. I honestly couldn't have found it if I tried, but there it was and there was a Girl Scout table out in front. I noticed from a distance a few of the coveted gluten free bags sitting on the table and quickly moved to purchase them. I was delighted with my prize stash, slipped them into my cooler and headed to the beach, astonished that my strong desire for those cookies had somehow led me right to them.

The stronger your desire for the "be, do, and have" wants on your list, the more likely your wandering paths will lead to your WOW.

Remember to focus on your feelings and strengthen them as you review your list daily.

When you change your focus to this positive vision, it's easier to see how you can change your situation.

There was a recent article in the Houston Chronicle regarding how the government is going to require automakers to equip new cars with technology that lets cars warn each other if they are headed toward disaster. This game-changing technology is already becoming a reality. It has the potential to drastically cut collisions, deaths and injuries. Radio signals transmit information back and forth about the position of vehicles, where they are headed, and how fast they are traveling among other information. Then the drivers receive alarms or messages or in some cases, the car is actually programmed to react (i.e. automatically brake).

Automotive safety used to focus on how to make sure we survived accidents. Now, it has changed to how to prevent accidents in the first place. The automotive industry has learned that by changing the focus or the question, you can change the answers. It's true for you, too.

HOW'S YOUR FOCUS?

Are you stuck making progress in a work or personal area? What questions are you asking yourself? Are you getting the same answers? Try turning the questions around.

Consider a person who is bedridden from an accident or surgery. You could ask "what kind of things could they do to entertain themselves while they are bedridden?" and potential answers could be read, write, play games, watch tv, etc. If you change the question to be "how can we get them up and out of the bed and mobile?" the focus changes, and so will the answers.

It all comes back to the What I Really, Really Want conversation. Changing your focus from what you don't want (i.e. SOS) to what you do want (i.e. WOW) can help you change the ideas that come into your head, and produce positive self-talk.

I had a toy clown growing up that was plastic and filled with air. It had sand in the bottom so that when you punched it, the clown popped back up to standing. I have often compared myself to that clown, and many agree. No matter what is going on, I don't stay down for long. Usually, I am hopelessly optimistic.

But, when I took a recent horseback riding lesson, I fell into the negative mode. The instructor had me trot the horse around the arena for several laps. She wanted me to focus on keeping the horse going. According to her, I did an excellent job. But, according to me there were so many things I wasn't doing right. My heels weren't down in the stirrups and I leaned forward sometimes. When I finished my lesson I immediately started listing all of the things I could have done better and she asked me to stop. Sure, there were things I could improve on, but I had done exactly as I was instructed and I really had things under control. So, why was I focusing on all the things I did wrong?

It is natural behavior to point out the negatives instead of the positives. Even Olympic athletes fall into this trap, as highlighted in recent Olympic games interviews. The tiny extra hop on a vault finish or bent knees on a dive have to be moved past for exceptional performance going forward.

For the next week, I challenge you to focus on what you are doing right. Yes, there will be things you could improve on, and it's ok to keep those in mind. But be more focused on what is going right and remind yourself what is going right — gently changing the conversations in your head to be more positive.

Positive thinking is more than just being happy or having an upbeat attitude. Studies show that the impact on our work, health and life can create great value. Negative thoughts actually narrow our thinking while positive emotions like joy or contentment have been found to open up our mind to possibilities. At the end of the day, try writing down all the things that went right that day and how you influenced them to turn out that way. Making this a regular practice will influence your mindset in the right direction.

Having a "can-do" mentality will open up, and help you remain open, to possibilities.

 I remember reading a novel when I was young that started off with a woman heading into a publishing company for an interview. While she was waiting in the lobby for her appointment she overheard an executive ask his assistant to find a copy of an old magazine. The woman waiting to be interviewed ran to the elevator and headed to another suite on a different floor. She knew there was a doctor's office in the building and they typically harbor old magazines. She found the office, quickly looked through the magazines in their waiting room and found the one the executive had mentioned. She returned to the publishing company and handed the executive the magazine she had unearthed. Not surprisingly, she got the job on the spot! I always loved that story and wanted to be "that girl."

Several years ago, I found "that girl" in person while attending a national women's golf networking organization event at a golf resort outside of Austin, TX. One evening, my girlfriends and I were having dinner and playing a card game on the patio but it was starting to get a dark. I asked the waitress if she had any candles or other table lights. "I think they might have some in the restaurant next door," she said. "Let me see what I can do." In a few minutes she returned with several candles for our table.

When she took our drink order, I asked for a Diet Coke. She said they only had Diet Pepsi so I accepted it. But when it arrived, it tasted a bit strange. The waitress said she would get me a can, and quickly returned with a glass of ice and a can of Diet Coke. Now where did she find that when the restaurant didn't even serve it? Maybe the employee refrigerator, my friends and I joked.

Later, she asked us if she could get us anything else. I hopefully shouted out "chocolate," since it wasn't on the menu, but we were craving it. Her reply? "I'll see what I can do!" A few minutes later she came back with two pieces of dark chocolate cake for us to share. Maybe she got them from a party since there were a lot of celebrations going on at the resort. We never found out, but it tasted great, and even nicer, it was free!

I tried to think of something for her to find that would be a real challenge. I mean, really, this woman was resourceful, creative and up to any request. What wouldn't she be able to do? We weren't able to stump her. Of course, we left a huge tip and wrote a letter to her manager commending her on her service, attitude and amazing ingenuity.

Here's the lesson I want you to take from this ingenious waitress. No matter the situation you're presented, respond — in your head or out loud — with "let me see what I can do." It's so much more powerful than "no way, that's impossible." When something seems impossible, train yourself to reframe it into "not yet, but I'm on my way." This one small shift will make all the difference in your ability to get from SOS to WOW.

You're probably saying, "Ok, Margaret. It all sounds great, but no matter how hard I try, sometimes doubt starts creeping in." Do your best to remain confident and trust that you are on the right path. Here's a story that might help.

 I worked in technical sales in the oil and gas industry as a contract consultant after a steady career as an employee in the power industry. I loved the flexibility of my contractor schedule, varying from part time to full time each week depending on what I had going on at the time. It allowed me to take care of my growing boys, support my traveling husband, grow my consulting business, and teach fitness classes.

One of the salesmen I worked with advised me to raise my contract rate every year. I had always been an employee before, receiving annual reviews and raises on a regular basis. So I never had to ask for a raise ... or should I say I never thought of asking for a raise outside of those constricts. Asking for a raise was something I knew I should do, but I wasn't familiar with the process. I started by writing out all of the reasons I deserved a raise, to back-up the amount I was planning on asking for. My salesman friend said, "you don't need a list of why you deserve a raise, you just go in there and ask for it!" He made it sound so simple and logical. I kept vacillating between justifying and just doing it, and finally I wrote a brief letter stating my new rate effective January 1.

I walked into the executive's office and presented my letter to him after briefly stating my reason for being there. He opened and read the letter, his mouth gaped open with shock, and then he looked up at me and casually said "ok." And that was it.

Wow! How many times do we hold ourselves back from the things we deserve or new things we want to try by doubting ourselves? It does always help to have a backup plan (some justification, analysis or research), but don't paralyze yourself with the process. I've said this before, and I'll say it again. Ask and (more often than not), you shall receive.

As I suggested earlier in this chapter, remind yourself of all the times things have worked out, gone right, or turned out positive. If you're not already doing so, now's a good time to start keeping a "joy" journal to reinforce your new positive mindset and the idea that all is possible.

Start right now. What are three things that went right today? List them here or directly in your joy journal.

1.

2.

3.

What will you do to form the habit of reflecting on things that are going well, and do it on a regular basis?

Another factor with the potential to undermine your positive mindset is your subconscious beliefs. I have an entrepreneurial client who, like most of us, has experienced some ups and downs over the course of her career. She was very successful, but at times would enter a phase where everything seemed to be falling apart. Eventually she would get herself together again and create new successes. Still, it seemed that every time she was about to reach a new height she would procrastinate and miss out on an important opportunity to grow her business. She really didn't know why she was sabotaging herself this way, and wanted to stop. As I worked with her to understand what was going on subconsciously, she revealed beliefs regarding women and success that had been ingrained in her since her childhood. She didn't realize those internalized beliefs were behind her inaction. But by identifying those subconscious limiting beliefs and addressing the truth regarding her capabilities she was finally able to move ahead and eliminate the success/failure roller coaster.

What can you do when this kind of thing happens to you? Check in with yourself and brainstorm a short list of beliefs you hold that might be affecting the situation. If that's not enough, work with a professional coach to reveal these possibilities. Uncovering your subconscious beliefs and replacing them with a new reality can be the key to getting your mindset truly in the positive mode. It is an ongoing process, but I promise it is very possible.

As you work to move from SOS to WOW, remember to eliminate the negative self-talk. Stay open to the possibilities and the belief that what you *do want* is possible.

CHAPTER 11

KEEP ON TRUCKIN'

MOVING IT ALL FORWARD

It's time to take stock of your progress. Moving forward involves noticing both what you've accomplished, and what else lies ahead.

Achievements are easy to acknowledge when they're particularly noticeable, like a brilliant sunset in Hawaii. I noticed this one day on vacation as the sun gently lowered in the sky toward the horizon. The beachgoers started gathering near the shore with their phones, cameras and other picture-taking devices in hand. Seemingly sinking ever so slowly into the sea, everyone's attention was drawn toward it. With a blink and a flash it was gone; the surrounding sky displayed beautiful shades of orange, red, yellow and clear blue in celebration of the sun's setting. In full appreciation of the experience, applause arose from the crowd of onlookers, as if to say, "good job God!" The thing is, though, even when it's obscured by clouds or rain, the sun rising and setting day after day is something to appreciate. The same is true for your accomplishments on the journey to WOW.

We are all at different stages on our SOS to WOW path and no matter where we are, celebrations are a vital part of the process. As you've worked through the chapters of this book, you've undoubtedly experienced some success. Acknowledging your effort, and the journey you are on, is a critical part of your continued success. No matter the size of the success, it's important to stop and appreciate how far you've come. Celebrations can provide you with a renewed spirit to continue ... and noticing where you currently reside will also provide you with a new benchmark from which to move forward. You've reached Step Three in my From SOS to WOW! model. WOW! It's time to celebrate.

What does celebrating progress look like?

As a writer, I've progressed from writing articles and blogs to self-help books, and I want to continue to expand into novels. Every time I make progress, I celebrate with champagne and friends. When my yogis and I hear a squeal of delight in the yoga room or see someone perform a pose that we can't even imagine trying that day, we celebrate along with them, sometimes even breaking into applause. As a coach, I acknowledge the work of my clients — the successes they experience personally and professionally — and partner with them to build on those successes to keep growing. If they are not typically in the habit of celebrating, as many are not, we work to create their personal habit of acknowledgment and celebration. The way you choose to celebrate your success is entirely up to you; just remember to take the time to do it.

What have you accomplished that deserves to be celebrated?

How will you celebrate?

How will you continue to incorporate celebrations into your journey?

BOUNCING BACK FROM SETBACKS

As we follow along our path with successes, we'll likely also experience some setbacks. Situations that we haven't anticipated may throw us for a temporary loop. Here is a story, and some advice to help you move forward through these times.

There is a place fairly near my house called the Sylvan Rodriguez Park. My favorite part of the park is the labyrinth that overlooks the lake. It is a brick laden path, winding back and forth within a circle that ultimately leads to the center. There are no dead ends like a typical maze. As people walk, they navigate turns that take them in different directions. Upon reaching the center, they follow the path back out.

There is something about the center. I have walked the labyrinth many times at different speeds and every time, when I arrive in the center I always pause and reflect. Sometimes it's to enjoy the view of the sun setting over the fields, other times to settle my head from the back and forth motion of switching directions constantly if I traversed the labyrinth at warp speed that day. Sometimes there is a cool lifting feeling, similar to the one you get when you set down your weights after several exerting repetitions at the gym. Sometimes it is just the quiet. Regardless of the draw, I always stand there with a feeling of accomplishment, even though the maze is not a competition.

Your journey to WOW is a lot like a labyrinth. The path you take will wind back and forth, but remember and realize that every step you take along it means you are making progress. From one day to the next you'll undoubtedly experience varying degrees of success. If you are working on a healthier stronger body, you might not start out feeling very strong or flexible. As you continue to practice you'll gain in each of those areas. And still, some days you'll feel slightly tight or have no strength.

If speaking in front of a group is your SOS, slowly mastering the skills of public speaking will be a journey with ups and downs. No matter what you are working on, there will be some days when it feels like you have gone completely backwards and lost a large part of what you worked so hard to gain. Be patient with yourself! Remaining steady on the path will ultimately bring you to your reward.

Part of being able to cope and succeed is the knowledge that temporary setbacks may — and probably will happen, and the more ready you are for them and the stronger your support system, the better you'll do.

I once attended an afternoon workshop on defining and working with all the resources available to move one's personal development or business forward. It was an interesting reminder to look at all we have around us, and pay attention to things that we typically forget or pass over as we rush through our week. We were asked to strive to make a list of 100 resources that we have, and were given a few minutes to complete the task. Pens and fingers on tablets moved furiously, listing person after person and item after item. Most people had 30 or more resources listed in a very short time. We shared part of our lists with the group and the ideas from others in the room inspired us to add to our lists, moving us closer to the individual goal of 100. In addition to all of the people I consider a resource and a blessing, I mentioned clutter to the group. Now, I'm not suggesting you hold onto all of your clutter, but sometimes the long-forgotten boxes stuffed away in our attics or under a bed hold treasures that could be used in our work or in some other way we hadn't previously considered.

The knowledge you've acquired, the friends you have, and the business contacts you've made at networking events are all part of your support network. In addition, if you consider the "stuff" you have in your head and home you will discover even more resources. For the "mental stuff," consider your experience, knowledge, training and the lessons you've learned throughout life and what could be applied to your current situation. For the "physical stuff," examine your book shelves and files (electronic and even paper if they still exist in your world) in your home and business offices. What resources do you have in the books you've purchased and the materials from the seminars and events you've attended?

So many resources around us get ignored or forgotten. Play with ways to utilize and engage with them differently. It's not always necessary to search for something new. You may have everything you need to support you now. You just need to perceive it in a different way.

What support systems do you have or will you need to put in place? Make a list of all of the resources that are available to support you in your journey to WOW.

Engage your friends in a brainstorming session to see how many each of you can add to your list.

Write at least one way you will engage with a resource you'd forgotten and how it will positively impact your success.

The ideas for engagement and the resources available to us are endless. I encourage you to enjoy and make better use of the old treasures in your proverbial closet. Continue to add new ones to grow your support system stockpile.

DON'T STOP HERE; KEEP SETTING A NEW WOW GOAL

Remember, WOW stands for Well On the Way, not done. As we work toward where we want to be, our current state of being changes and we move closer to where we want to end up. As you progress with your health, relationships, career or dreams, your vision of where you want to be transforms. My advice to you is to continue setting new WOWs to keep yourself motivated and engaged in continuous personal growth. In reality, we are never finished; we are always on our way to becoming the masterpiece we are meant to be.

Reflecting on where you are now, what is your next WOW? Write it down and get ready to re-start your SOS to WOW journey. You've reached the final step in my From SOS to WOW! model. Onward and Upward! Congratulations!

CHAPTER 12

ENJOY THE RIDE

LIFE IS A JOURNEY

I was recently reminded of the old adage to "stop and smell the roses" when my son sent me a picture of his vacation in Denver. He was leaning over to smell the roses in a garden, something he said he'd never done before, and I wanted to share this next story as a reminder to you to enjoy your SOS to WOW journey. We are on a joyful journey, a lifelong adventure to new and better places for ourselves and our world. Don't just focus on the end result.

 The Road to Hana is an incredible day trip full of water-falls, underwater caves, trails, and black sand beaches — definitely not to be missed by those visiting the island of Maui. It is recommended that you start your trip with a visit to a little convenience store on the corner to pur-chase a self-guided tour on CD, load up on snacks and

drinks, and jump in your car. If you skip that step you might miss the whole point of the Road to Hana.

It is a delightful day full of frequent stops to enjoy scenic event after event, some quite adventurous. They involve climbing, traipsing along a trail, jumping into an underwater cave or just standing by a rushing waterfall enjoying the roar and the mist. Some adventures are not for the light of heart. I've witnessed many people standing on the shore watching the crazier ones daring the waves to crash over them and knock them over.

Once you reach Hana you are cautioned to turn around and head back in the opposite direction of how you arrived because the road ahead on the back side of the island can be lonely and treacherous. The car rental companies declare in no uncertain terms that they will not rescue you if you decide to ignore the warnings and continue your way around the prohibited side of the island. "Ah, let's do it," my husband smiled. I guess my silence was interpreted as yes. And so we did do it. Granted, some turns were a little "hairy" with seemingly nothing but the air between us and the ocean. Once in a while we saw another car but they were very few and very far between. A few curves made me hold my breath but he was very careful and we were never in any real danger. My concern was reaching civilization again before the sun set so we could see where we were going as those mountain turns were no place to be in the dark. We did discover a winery hidden in the hills and vowed to return the next day to check it out (from the opposite direction — the safer direction). We made it home to our hotel safe and sound that night. And yes, we did return to the winery the next day for a delightful wine tasting.

"Hana?" a friend exclaimed as I detailed our trip on our return. "I drove to Hana and it wasn't all that spectacular — what is all the hoopla about?" he asked.

"Did you stop at the little party store and pick up the CD," I asked him. "Did you stop along the way to see the waterfalls, the black sand beach, the underwater caves, the forest trails?" I added to my questions. All his answers were "no."

"Then you missed it all" I lamented. "It is not Hana itself, but the Road to Hana that is so heavenly."

I invite you to enjoy your journey From SOS to WOW! Just like the Road to Hana, you will experience joy, and wonder and a bit of fear as you venture into unfamiliar territory. Take delight in each step along the way. Know that you are making progress and that your WOW may change ... and that is ok. It is all good because we are never really done. We are always WOW — Well

On the Way — to being where we want to be and each step and stop along the way must be celebrated and enjoyed for what it is ... bringing us one step closer to something I call SWOW.™

What is SWOW? It's when you are SO Well On the Way to where you want to be. I coined the acronym one day when I was feeling especially great, enjoying a record crowd for my "Managing Up! Bossing the Boss" presentation at a project management conference. A friend asked me how I felt and I replied "Wow!" Then I repeated the expression slowly with a "Soooo" preceding the "Wow!" and the shortcut term SWOW was born. It was an incredible feeling of deserving, enjoying life, and being in the place with my personal and professional life that I was meant to be in. It truly felt great. And I invite you to adopt it. SWOW is exuding confidence, swagger, and experiencing the feeling that motivates and inspires you to keep moving forward in the direction you need and want to flow. It is the ultimate feeling of confidence and joy, where all is right in your world as you stay open to the possibilities.

Regularly reviewing the steps outlined in this book will continue to bring you to SWOW:

- ▶ Evaluating your area for change—SOS;

- ▶ Visualizing a more effective and productive mode of operating—WOW;

- ▶ Recognizing and capitalizing on your motivation;

▸ Focusing on one task at a time and avoiding the pitfalls of multitasking;

▸ Assessing where you are making assumptions, how you are holding yourself back, and how you will remove those barriers to progress;

▸ Keeping your mind open to possibilities through creative techniques;

▸ Examining the risks involved in making changes and adjusting the approach for more successful results; and

▸ Keeping a mind-set of positivity and focus on what you want to achieve and not what you want to avoid.

Stay curious and open to "what if" and the possibilities that question presents. Here's to you and your SWOW!

I'd love to hear about your successes! Here are four ways to be in touch:

▸ Tweet SWOW successes to me.
  @sidekickcoach #SWOW

▸ Post on Facebook.
  www.facebook.com/IdealTrainingInc

▸ Comment on my blog.
  igniteyourideas.blogspot.com

▸ Send me an email.
  margaret@ideasandbeyond.com

ADDITIONAL CHALLENGES AND TECHNIQUES

APPENDIX

WHAT'S HERE?

▸ 21-Day Risk Taking Challenge

▸ Breathe, Just Breathe! — Breathing Exercises

▸ Creativity Resources

▸ Space for writing Ideas for Unleashing My Creative Genius

21-DAY RISK TAKING CHALLENGE — ARE YOU IN?

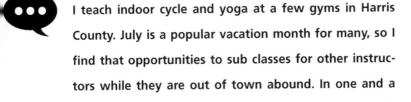 I teach indoor cycle and yoga at a few gyms in Harris County. July is a popular vacation month for many, so I find that opportunities to sub classes for other instructors while they are out of town abound. In one and a half weeks, I taught a total of ten cycling classes, which

is well above my normal twice a week workload. Before the craziness began, I invited members and Facebook friends to join in a challenge to take all ten classes with me. Several people accepted the challenge, and a few actually were able to attend all ten.

When I arrived in the cycling room the last evening to teach that tenth class, I noticed a case of water bottles with a card attached to it near my bike on the instructor platform. I always bring a cooler of cold water bottles to class for those who forget or run out of water, and someone had thoughtfully gifted me a whole case. I didn't have a chance to open the card until after class and was delighted to read this message: *"Dear Margaret, Challenge Completed! Thanks for encouraging me to do something I didn't think I could do. You're awesome."*

Actually, I think she is the awesome one, not me. And I delight in her success. She stretched herself beyond her comfort zone and found strength she didn't know she had. What do you think will happen for her now? I foresee her taking more risks and accepting more challenges and continuing to grow.

If you would like to continue to expand yourself beyond your comfort zone and experience a little more WOW in your life, take my 21-Day Risk Challenge. Each day, review that day's challenge.

You can accept it, modify it, or reject it and make up your own. The important thing is to take some type of risk every day. Make a note under each challenge to track what risk you took. At the end of 21 days, reflect on your experience. What have you learned about yourself or what has changed in you for the better?

Let me know what came out of this experience for you by

- posting on my Facebook page (www.facebook.com/IdealTrainingInc/)

- tweeting (@sidekickcoach #risktaker) or

- emailing me (margaret@ideasandbeyond.com).

You will be amazed at the difference taking even small risks can do for your confidence, self-esteem, and your enthusiasm for life.

Day 1 — Try some type of exercise that you've never tried before. You can go to a class at a studio, gym, park or look up some exercises on the Internet. It can be as simple as jumping rope, a walk in the park, the hula hoop or a new dance step — whatever you choose.

Day 2 — Tell a stranger something nice about them that you observed. If you are in the grocery line and notice something about the person in front of you or behind you — let them know (positive things)! Approach someone new at a business networking event or other public place. If this isn't a stretch for you, how could you modify this challenge to make it one?

Day 3 — Ask for what you need or want. One of my friends wanted to work in the Paris, France (not Texas!) office of the company she worked for but never let management know that was her desire. She hinted toward it but never outright asked or told them her goal. So — what happened? She's not in Paris. Ask for what you need or want — they don't know if you don't let them know.

Day 4 — Let go of something you know isn't serving you anymore. Is it work files that you hold onto that you think you might need someday, or some other clutter at home? Is it a relationship that you keep tolerating when that person is annoying you or not treating you very well? It might be time to let it go.

Day 5 — Reach out to someone you admire but are afraid to talk to. I frequently hear clients say that they admire someone at work at a high level or saw an article about someone who had taken action and was living the dream they had for themselves. Reach out to that person. Let them know what you admire about them. It may be exactly what they needed to hear and you may hear back exactly what you need to hear.

Day 6 — Go home from work on time. Don't stay late. Is it possible for you? If you are an entrepreneur, don't do any work after 5:00pm. What do you notice? What are you afraid will happen if you don't keep working late? Is it really true?

Day 7 — Say "that something" that really needs to be said.
I miss The Tonight Show with Jay Leno but have been and continue to give Jimmy Fallon a chance. I watched it the other night because a favorite of mine, Meryl Streep, was a guest. Jimmy asked her questions but never let her reply; he answered for her or talked over her while she was talking. He does it frequently. I posted on the Tonight Show with Jimmy Fallon Facebook page and trust the message will get through to the right people. Say what's on your mind — tactfully and professionally. You'll feel better about yourself and, hopefully, make a difference.

Day 8 — Say no. Are you overwhelmed with a full schedule? Pay attention to what you really need and what will bring you joy, and don't be afraid to say no to overbooking.

Day 9 — Try a new look. Cut or color you hair a new way. Shave your mustache. Try a new style or color of clothing. One of my girlfriends almost always wore black to the gym. She wore a colorful shirt one day after years of her old pattern. What a difference. Give it a try. It will have pleasant rippling effects.

Day 10 — Do it differently. Take a different route to work, manage a meeting differently, take a risk and change a habit — a little or drastically.

Day 11 — Check out a different crowd. Attend the organizational meeting of a group you don't typically associate with. My husband and I went to a sports bar called Quaker Steak and Lube for a Green Bay Packers game against the Vikings. We are Viking fans and were the only ones with Vikings jerseys on in a sea of Cheeseheads. We met a lot of new friends and had a great time.

Day 12 — Turn off your cell phone for a day. See what you've been missing. What are you afraid of if you really do it? Try it for an hour if a day is too much of a challenge. You will be amazed at what you see and hear that you were missing before. Notice the difference in the people around you who are now getting your devoted attention, and how you can really connect.

Day 13 — Speak up when you see something wrong and do something about it. I am ready to write a letter to Chevy. In their latest commercial they promote a screen on the dashboard with text responses to select from — to respond to incoming texts you listen to from your phone that is connected by blue tooth. They think this will help people keep their eyes on the road. I think it is a big mistake and will write to them and let them know. What will you speak up about today?

Day 14 — Ask for feedback from someone on how you are doing. Ask your boss or your kids or your significant other — or anyone you can think of — for feedback on these three questions:

1.   What am I doing that you like and want me to keep doing?

2. What am I doing that you don't like and want me to stop doing?

3. What am I not doing that you would like me to start doing?

I think you will be pleasantly surprised about their thoughts.

Day 15 — Sign up for something new. Take a class you've always wanted to take or sign up to start a degree program at a community college or university. Sign up to rescue an animal. Sign up to be the chairman of an organization. Sign up to volunteer for a charitable organization. Whatever gets you excited. Sign up! Get started.

Day 16 — Take the first step toward a goal you've always wanted but you've been procrastinating on. What is it? If your goal is to get a promotion at work, the first step is asking for more responsibility. If you want to lose weight, the first step may be joining an exercise or weight loss group. If you want to be a writer, the first step might be submitting an article to a magazine for publication. Take that step today.

Day 17 — Admit you don't know. Do you stay quiet in class when the professor asks if there are any questions? Do you hesitate to ask a question in a meeting at work because you are worried it is a dumb question? Admit when you don't know. There is always more to learn.

Day 18 — Do something you want to do, but don't think you can do. Remember the challenge I posed to my cycle members in the story at the beginning? I challenged friends and gym members to do ten classes in ten days. Some didn't think they could but were inspired and motivated to accomplish it. One of my clients had a co-worker who was always asking for help with her work and slyly sloughing the work off on her. My client wanted to stand up to her but didn't think she could. Through coaching, she was able to and the co-worker is doing her part now. Do something you don't think you can do.

Day 19 — Accept a challenge. The obstacles you are afraid of aren't likely to materialize. I played the song "Mustang Sally" one night in indoor cycle class. I challenged the class to turn their dial to the right, adding resistance and therefore more hill to their workout every time the artist, Wilson Pickett, sang the words "Mustang Sally." "Are you in," I asked. I received a less than enthusiastic response though some signaled they were up to the challenge. Guess what? The phrase "Ride Sally Ride" is sung quite a bit more in the song than "Mustang Sally," which is only repeated a few times. So the numerous extra turns of the dial my class was afraid of never materialized.

And so it is with the risks we avoid in life. Like I said in Chapter 9, so often we imagine all of the obstacles we will come up against, and many of them never happen. And, if they do, remember that you are more than capable of handling them. So take on the challenge. Take a chance. Do it! You'll be fine.

Day 20 — Wow, you're almost there! Make the call you've been procrastinating about. Do you need to follow up on a resume you sent in response to a job posting? Is there someone you've wanted to ask out and you haven't yet? Do you need to call up a friend with a serious illness but don't know what to say, so you haven't called? Do you need to tell someone you love them? Make the call today.

Day 21!!! — You did it — congratulations! The risk for today is to scare yourself (just a little bit). Do whatever it is that will push you a little beyond your comfort zone and scare you just a bit. Make it a daily habit from now on.

What did you learn about yourself as you went through the 21-day risk taking challenge?

What has changed for the better?

What will you continue to do moving forward as a result of this experience?

BREATHE, JUST BREATHE — BREATHING EXERCISES

A group of friends signed up for a 5K evening race, called the Neon Splash Dash. Even though I hadn't run that distance in quite some time, being a night owl, it seemed like my kind of race, so I signed up too. The start area was packed with close to 10,000 runners wearing white t-shirts that would be sprayed with neon paint on the course, and everything was decorated with all varieties of neon flashing and glowing gadgets. It was very cool.

It took some time for the waves of runners/walkers to move forward so that we finally reached the starting line, and the adrenaline was definitely pumping through my veins. At last, we were off! I found a clear spot and reached a rhythmic pace. But about ten minutes later I had to slow down to ease a mild pain in my side, most likely from not breathing correctly. I focused on correcting my breath work and picked up the pace again. In doing so, I was able to finish strong and my starting group of familiar faces — now splattered with paint — was not far behind.

I use breathing techniques all the time, but that didn't mean I automatically remembered them, and it didn't make me immune to needing them as I ran that race. It's one thing to have knowledge of something, and a whole other to use it. Remember, whether you are running a race, working on a pose in yoga, about to stand up and speak to a crowd, or getting ready to have a difficult conversation with someone, it's the breath underneath it all that makes it successful. Use your breath to relax and get in the right frame of mind, and everything will be easier.

Practice these breathing exercises and find opportunities in your daily work and personal life to make use of them:

Find a comfortable place to sit either on a mat or in a comfortable chair, with your hips slightly raised above your knees and your arms relaxed in your lap. You may keep your eyes open or closed. Be sure to breathe in and out through your mouth with your lips closed for each exercise. Try each exercise for a few minutes and build up to 10-15 minutes each time, aiming for a habit of practicing one every day.

▶ **Simple In & Out** — as you breathe in, focus on the word "in," slowing and deepening the breath as much as you can. Pause for a second. As you exhale, focus on the word "out," slowing and deepening the breath as much as you can. Pause for a second and repeat the cycle 5 times or more, depending what you need and have time for.

▶ **Countdown** — as you breathe in and out, try to slow down and deepen the breath with each inhale and exhale, and silently count down backwards from 200. If you get lost and forget where you were, start back at 200.

▶ **Four corners** — as you breathe in and out, with your eyes closed, focus on the corners of an imaginary square. As you breathe in for four counts, set your gaze on the upper left corner of the square. Move your eyes to the upper right corner of the square and hold your breath for four counts. Move your eyes to the bottom right corner and exhale for four. Slide your eyes over to the lower left corner of the square and hold for four counts. Repeat the cycle.

▶ **Breath Holding** — take a breath in quickly and deeply to the count of four, hold the breath for a count of 16, (don't hold your breath if you are pregnant or have high blood pressure), then release the breath for a count of 8. Repeat.

Any time you are anxious, need to relax, or want to meditate for a few minutes, practice one of these breathing exercises. Calmness and focus will be your reward.

CREATIVITY RESOURCES

Chapter 8, Unleashing Your Creative Genius, is chock full of tips and techniques to increase your creativity. If you are interested in researching the topic further, here are a few of my favorite books on the subject:

▶ *Business Innovation for Dummies* by Alexander Hiam

▶ *Creativity Workout — 62 Exercises to Unlock Your Most Creative Ideas* by Edward De Bono

▶ *Cracking Creativity — The Secrets of Creative Genius* by Michael Michalko

310 FROM SOS TO WOW!

▸ *Creative Thinkering — Putting Your Imagination to Work* by Michael Michalko

▸ *Thinkertoys — A Handbook of Creative-Thinking Techniques* by Michael Michalko (can you tell I really like this guy's work?!)

▸ *Voice of the Innovator — How the Voice of the Innovator Can Be Cultivated in Individuals, Teams, and Organizations* by Jacqueline Byrd

Ideas for Unleashing My Creative Genius:

Ideas for Unleashing My Creative Genius:

ABOUT THE AUTHOR

MARGARET A. JOHNSON, P.E.

Margaret A. Johnson grew up in Detroit, Michigan and moved to Texas as fast as she could after graduating from Michigan State University. She utilizes her B.S. Mechanical Engineering, MBA, professional engineering license and coaching credentials to inspire people and organizations to move from SOS (Same Old Stuff) to WOW! Johnson's experience ranges from engineering and management in the electric power industry to sales and consulting in the oil and gas industry. As President of Ideal Training, Inc., she trains and coaches professionals with a mission to unleash creativity, ignite ideas and remove barriers to success to assist clients in solving problems and opening doors, and to keep her leadership and fitness classes engaging.

Creator of the SWOW! movement — taking people from SOS to WOW and joyfully being SWOW (So Well On the Way to where they want to be), she takes great pleasure in spreading that SWOW feeling to all through coaching, training, writing, and speaking.

Margaret resides in Friendswood, Texas, with her husband. Their two sons, Jeff and Michael, and their fiancées (respectively Hilary and Chrissy) live in the greater Houston area.

CONTACT MARGARET FOR ADDITIONAL SWOW ASSISTANCE

▶ Coaching services on getting yourself or your organization from SOS to WOW!

▶ Training on assumption busting, creativity and risk taking

▶ An inspiring and motivating keynote speaker

Contact her: margaret@ideasandbeyond.com

For more information visit **www.ideasandbeyond.com.**

SHOW OFF
YOUR SWOW

Keep that WOW feeling with SWOW Swag. SWOW (So Well on the Way) merchandise including t-shirts may be purchased online at **www.ideasandbeyond.com**.

Additional copies of *From SOS to WOW! Your Personal Coaching Adventure* may be purchased online at **Amazon.com**, in local bookstores, or at in-person events with Margaret Johnson.

For more information visit **www.ideasandbeyond.com**.

Made in the USA
Columbia, SC
17 April 2017